#BEWORTHFOLLOWING: How to Be Different and Influence People in a Crowded Social World

#BEWORTHFOLLOWING: How to Be Different and Influence People in a Crowded Social World

Dr. Jennifer Bennett

Table of Contents

●●●●●●●

Part I: First Things First · 1
　Chapter 1: #BeSocial · 3
　Chapter 2: #BeGod's · 11
　Chapter 3: #BeHealthy · 22
　Chapter 4: #BeGiving · 33

Part II: Building Blocks · 41
　Chapter 5: #BeDifferent · 43
　Chapter 6: #BeReal · 55
　Chapter 7: #BeMissional · 68
　Chapter 8: #BeDiscerning · · · · · · · · · · · · · · · · · · 78

Part III: Growing Pains · 87
　Chapter 9: #BeEnduring · 89
　Chapter 10: #BePractical · · · · · · · · · · · · · · · · · · 106
　Chapter 11: #BeCreative · · · · · · · · · · · · · · · · · · · 114

Part IV: Working Above the High Bar · · · · · · · · · · · · 121
　Chapter 12: #BeClear · 123
　Chapter 13: #BeFearless · · · · · · · · · · · · · · · · · · · 133
　Chapter 14: #BeSuccessful · · · · · · · · · · · · · · · · 147

Foreword

Just this week I saw a quote (online of course) that said, "We used to go online to escape the world and now we go into the world to escape online!" And how true that is! Our lives have slowly migrated from the multi-dimensional world into the flatly-dimensional world that is social media.

Our friends meet in Facebook chat or groups instead of for coffee. Our prayer requests are shared with a status update and acknowledged by clicks, hearts and sad-faced emojis instead of hugs, voices and knowing nods.

Instead of measuring our words carefully to protect our relationships, we use our social profiles as soap boxes and stumps in which to shout our opinion, share our non-fact-checked fake news, rant about politics and brag about our families. We do carefully choose NOT to share the D on the report card, the call from the principal's office or the broken engagement, unless we are seeking sympathy, therapy or shaming.

Worse yet, we have begun to place our value on how many likes, shares, emojis, comments or new friends we gain. We are in a moment-by-moment race for validation about every decision, emotion, activity, episode or photo. Heaven help us!

What a complex place, social media. It is the most connective and simultaneously divisive medium I've seen.

And yet, I have hope. I have hope that we can choose our friends as carefully online as off. That we can carefully choose whom to listen to and who to engage in discourse with. I have hope we can be a light in a dark world and salt in a bland one. I have hope we can use our everyday influence to share product knowledge, hacks and tips, encouraging moments and resources with one another. I have hope we can stay connected with missionaries, military and a mobile work force. I have hope we can share the joy of Jesus, the hope of Christ and God's sovereign love in a way that transcends the single dimension of the screen's glow.

Jen knows I'm passionate about social media. I'm connected to people globally whom I seek to encourage, empower and even entertain. I don't apologize for my convictions, but I don't seek to debate, either. I choose to focus on positive and show others how to do the same. I save hard topics for folks I have relationship capital with. I use my influence carefully, weighing the cost of each directive. Every day I'm choosing to walk on sunshine, not eggshells. Jesus is the light of the world. It is my job to reflect that light. Online and off.

And because of social media, I met Dr. Jen. Her message is timely, it's weighty and it's needed. Women are especially prone to the comparison trap, the gossip gauntlet and the mask-wearing. We are also prone to getting sucked into time-stealers, and social media can literally take your entire day and sleep time too!

This book will help. Dr. Jen's heart for ministry, for women and for media is woven together beautifully into a message that the Kingdom needs now more than ever.

Read this with a highlighter. Turn off your media for a few days. Pray for wisdom and discernment and trust my friend as the Lord speaks through her.

And then ... I'll see you online!

Carrie Wilkerson
CarrieWilkerson.com
Author. Speaker. Consultant.

Part I:
First Things First

●●●●●●●

What is meant by laying the right foundation for social-media success? What can social media offer your business or ministry? What do you need to be willing to do for success online? All these questions and more are a great start. Welcome to #BeWorthFollowing!

Chapter 1: #BeSocial
Why Do I Need Social Media?

Make a careful exploration of who you are and the work you have been given, and then sink yourself into that. Don't be impressed with yourself. Don't compare yourself with others. Each of you must take responsibility for doing the creative best you can with your own life.
Galatians 6:4–5, MSG

Let's get right to the point: Why social media?

I'm taking an educated guess that you chose this book because you either 1) are a leader in business or ministry and want to know how to utilize social media to its highest potential, or 2) you aspire to those goals and want to know how to utilize social media to its highest potential—so you can reach yours.

Am I getting close? Great, we're all in good company. I started from the ground up with social media, and every day I seek to make the most of my online presence so that I can help women thrive in their God-given dreams.

So let's start at the beginning and talk about those dreams. If our point is to make the most of our online efforts, then we first need to understand who we are and what our ultimate goal is.

If we are trying to garner attention or build our platform, well, there may be a nugget of value in starting there. But what makes this book different from advice you'll find from many other social-media experts is the focus on working from a foundation and toward success *based on God and the dreams he puts in our hearts.*

That focus on God makes all the difference for our businesses, our ministries, and the rest of our lives. Keeping God as our primary focus is how we start to #BeWorthFollowing. We'll get to more of that soon, just as we'll cover lots of practical tools for how to make your online investment count.

But first, let's take a look at some key answers to that very first question: Why social media? No matter what kind of business or ministry you're in, social media is a necessary component of your marketing strategy. More and more businesses and ministries are realizing how important social media is to their online success.

A 2015 Pew Research poll showed that 65 percent of adults use social networking, which is ten times more than the previous decade. And as of 2014, the gap between statistics of women and men users has been closing, with 68 percent of women and 62 percent of men utilizing social media.

It's not a question of *if* but *when* you should start getting social. Here's why.

8 Reasons to focus on social media

1. You can connect with your ideal client.
More and more people are getting active on social media, and what's even better is that these active users are providing a plethora of information about who they are, what they like and don't like, and what they need. There has never been a better time to find and connect with your ideal client.

2. Your tribe wants to connect with you.
Yes, your tribe wants to connect with YOU! They want to get to know the face behind the business and ministry. They want to

know you as a person. They want to be in community with you! The more you build this and allow them in, the more they will want to connect and engage with you.

3. Social media provides solutions.

Have you noticed that people are asking questions on social media? Not only are they Googling their questions, they're also asking their social networks for recommendations, ideas, and referrals. Their questions give you tremendous insight into the needs of your tribe. The more active you are on your platforms, the more likely you are to see those questions and understand your audience—and as a bonus, you're more likely to be recommended as the answer to someone's question.

4. It's cost effective.

Social media gives you the opportunity to build brand awareness and influence like never before. Prior to social media, businesses and ministries had to pay a pretty penny for advertising in magazines, newspapers, TV and radio spots. But today, for just a few dollars a day, you can create a brand awareness with the potential to reach millions. You have the opportunity to reach large numbers of people by simply being active on social media!

5. Social media is a source of referrals.

I don't know about you, but when I'm looking for someone who can help me with a question or issue, I always ask for referrals on social media. Need a house cleaner? Let me ask my social-media friends who they've used and recommended. Need a pediatrician? Who have my friends used and loved? Social media will provide referrals for your business—all you have to do is ask. When your clients know your character and who you are as a person, they will be more likely to refer more clients to you.

6. Customer service is everything.

People are increasingly looking to social media to have their customer service needs met. And many businesses are not doing it well. Why? Because they're still using social media as a broadcaster. They post when they feel like it and it's all about their products and services. Even worse, they never check back to see if anyone has engaged and is asking them questions that they can answer. But you have a unique opportunity to shine online as you help current and future clients with their questions about you, your products, and your services.

7. Social media is a research tool.

Social media can help you learn more about your tribe. Not only can you ask questions on your platforms, but you can see how your tribe interacts with your competitors and how your competitors are responding. It's never been easier to gain a solid understanding of what makes your tribe tick.

8. You can learn about the influencers in your niche.

Do you know who your competition is? Do you know what they're doing right? What they are doing wrong? What you can improve so that your business shines online? Social media gives you this opportunity to see, learn and improve upon what your competition is doing.

Sounds promising, right? We understand why we need to polish our social-media strategies. But we also need to ask some preliminary questions of ourselves to assess our readiness for the consistent and determined work it takes to build our presence online.

Soul searching

1. **Why do I want to use social media?** There has to be a bigger reason than just making sales and making money. Deep

down inside, why do you want to be social and why would people want to be social with you? What is your bigger *why* for social media?

2. **What does social-media success look like to me?** This is where you have to really think through and write down what success looks like to you, not what it looks like to everyone else. What does success on social media look like for you in the next six months? Year? Three years? Five years? Don't be afraid to create a success plan that fits with who you are and your personal goals. God has given each of us a different path, a different journey, which means our definitions of success will look different.

3. **Do I have time for social media? If so, how much time?** Social media takes time; it's not a post-and-leave-it kind of platform. It requires daily commitment and interaction. This is where you have to get really honest with yourself. If you don't have time for social media, do you have the income to hire someone to help you? If you don't, then what one platform can you commit to (remember, you don't have to be on every platform)?

4. **Who is my target audience?** If there is one thing I want you to remember, it is this: You can't be all things to all people. When I first started out, this was a trap I soon found myself in. And because I was trying to be all things to all people, my messages, my posts, my stories never resonated with the right people. Knowing who your target audience is (your dream client) will help you cater everything you post on social media to them. And when you have a clear understanding of *who* they are, your messages will connect with them because you are writing to their hearts, to who they are as individuals.

5. **What is the main message that I want to share through social media?** I'm a big believer in that every leader, every entrepreneur, should have one main message that aligns with their mission, their business, and their values. This one message is what you will share on a regular basis. It's the message that you will become known for. This message could be your story, which we'll get to, or it could be a part of that story. The key here is that you have a main message that you share on a regular basis on social media.

As you already know, my main message is all about #BeWorthFollowing. Everything I do, post, and say revolves around this message. It's what I've become known for. And it's the same thing that you want to do for yourself, your business. What are you most passionate about? What moves you? What one big message do you want to share with the world? Your answer to these questions will help you create that one main message that you will share on social media.

We've got a good start—let's build on it! Speaking of building, any construction project that weathers the tests of time and the elements must have a good foundation. And so the case is with building our platforms, specifically online.

Tips from the front line

If you only have time to be on one social-media platform, then I recommend that it be Facebook. Why? It's the biggest and most popular social-media platform with over one billion active users. It's also the one platform that you can do the most with and the one platform that the majority of people feel the most comfortable with. The key here is that you have a Facebook Business Page. According to Facebook's Terms of Service, you cannot use a personal profile to conduct business. The advantages to having a Facebook page include

- advertising capabilities that allow you to really target your ideal clients;
- access to insights that include how many people your posts are reaching, age range of your community, where your likes are coming from, your most popular posts, etc.;
- the ability to include a call-to-action button that leads people to your website and gives you the opportunity to grow your list;
- the ability to sell from your page;
- unlimited "friends." Personal profiles are limited to 5,000 friends, but a Facebook page is unlimited in how many people can like it;
- the ability to run a Facebook Offer that allows you to promote a product, service, downloadable, etc., to your audience;
- the ability to assign a variety of roles to your page. These include an admin, editor, moderator, advertiser, analyst and a live contributor;
- the ability to schedule posts ahead of time using the Native Facebook Scheduler.

Questions to consider
1. What dreams has God already brought to fruition in my life?
2. What dreams has He planted in my heart that He's been telling me it's time to move forward on?
3. What is my goal for social media?
4. What challenges do you see ahead of you on social media?

Tweetable moments
"Focusing on God makes all the difference for our businesses, our ministries, and the rest of our lives." ~@DrJenBennett, #BeWorthFollowing

"Keeping God as our primary focus is how we start to #BeWorthFollowing." ~@DrJenBennett, #BeWorthFollowing

"When your clients know your character and who you are as a person, they will be more likely to refer more clients to you."
~@DrJenBennett, #BeWorthFollowing

"God has given each of us a different path, a different journey, which means our definitions of success will look different."
~@DrJenBennett, #BeWorthFollowing

"Knowing who your target audience is (your dream client) will help you cater everything you post on social media to them."
~@DrJenBennett, #BeWorthFollowing

"Every leader, every entrepreneur, should have one main message that aligns with their mission, their business, and their values."
~@DrJenBennett, #BeWorthFollowing

Chapter 2: #BeGod's
The Cornerstone of the Foundation

More than anything else, put God's work first and do what he wants.
                                                      Matthew 6:33, CEV

You already have an idea that social media should be a foundational part of your promotional strategy if you want to increase your brand awareness and influence. Taking a proactive approach is key, meaning we need to go where the people are. My friend, they are on social media.

If you long to make an impact offline, begin by making it online.

However, let's back up one important step. If we long to make the most influential impact *period*, we must begin with the right foundation. Let's see what that means.

Maintaining a God-focus leads to the health of everything else in our lives, including our business and ministry. Looking to God for our definition of success before we dive into building our platform (our tribe) makes all the difference in how we view our goals and how we will know what sort of impact we're making.

We'll talk more about true success later on, but for now let's invite God in to our ultimate purpose in life. Matthew 22:37–39 (NLT) says, "Jesus replied: 'Love the Lord your God with all your heart and with all your soul and with all your mind.' This is the first and greatest commandment. And the second is like it: 'Love your neighbor as yourself.'"

Notice how the primary commandment is to love God, even before loving others? Yes, He deserves our greatest love. That's the main point. But from that order, we can also see a second truth: When we love God first, we *are able to love* others, to focus on others. God must be first if we're to be rightly related to anyone or anything else in life.

One important question to ask ourselves every day is *Whose platform am I really building, my own or God's?*

Whose platform am I building, my own or God's?

Write it on a Post-It for your computer monitor. Make a selfie video on your phone so you can visually ask yourself this question every day. Set a consistent tone for your life by committing to make your business or ministry about building the Kingdom instead of creating your own kingdom, and watch how he brings opportunities your way to glorify him—and to provide for you and through you.

We'll discuss lots of practical tips for building our online presence. But first, let me tell you about the most practical step you can take each day. Keep an open mind, because at first glance it may not seem very practical at all—but that's short-sighted thinking.

Proactively meeting with God every day is the most practical step we can take toward a productive day and a social network that's as wide reaching as God desires for the work He gives us. You may already have a habit of daily quiet time with the Lord, or maybe you've heard of it and want to know its worth.

Why is a daily meeting with God so practical? Because it reminds us each day that we are working on his platform. We need his direction to keep him first, because our human nature is to promote ourselves more than him. Even the trend to be "on mission" can be warped into focusing on how much we want to do for him instead of seeing our weaknesses and limitations, our talents and successes in light of Him.

John 15:1–2 (MSG) says, "I am the Vine, you are the branches. When you're joined with me and I with you, the relation intimate and organic, the harvest is sure to be abundant. Separated, you can't produce a thing."

That's pretty straightforward! Think about the image of a branch growing from the vine. The vine provides the resources the branch needs to grow. Ah! We need to look daily to the Lord, to remain connected to Him, if we (and thus any of our efforts) are to grow strong and productive.

Our dreams come from the Lord. We may have lots of dreams for our lives, so how do we know which ones He wants us to run with? Well, through time in His Word, prayer, and rubbing shoulders with others who have the same main focus, eyes and hearts on Him.

Psalm 37:4 (ESV) says, "Delight yourself in the Lord, and he will give you the desires of your heart." It might be tempting to read that as if He will grant us every dream we ask Him for. But with some adjusting of our priorities to align them with His, we can read the verse's meaning to be that if we delight ourselves in the Lord, He will put His desires for us into our hearts—*He'll plant the desires into us that He wants to fulfill through us.* God dreamers don't trust their own voice and ideas; they trust the voice and ideas of God.

That truth is nothing short of miraculous—and He wants that personally for you and for me. He wants to work through us. Amen!

When you live and work keeping God as your focus, doors will open. Seek Him with every fiber of your being, continue being faithful to Him and opportunity will seek *you*. As it does, remember God brought you here, and He'll help keep you accountable for what you do with what He's given you.

Building a solid foundation

I want you to last. I want your business to last. I want your ministry to last. I want you to build a life and business/ministry that is not only pleasing to God, but one that that will last, even when the obstacles and challenges come your way.

But when it comes to being social on social media, we tend to come to it with the wrong mindset, a mindset that will not last.

Our initial thought is that social media is all about selling and making sales. The more we can push, promote and broadcast what it is that we have to offer, the more sales we will get, and in turn, the more successful we will be. But if this is the way we approach our businesses on social media, we will not last.

We have it backwards. Yes, social media allows us some great opportunities to connect with our dream clients, who in turn will want to do business with us. But the reality is, that comes much later.

All of this goes back to #BeWorthFollowing. Before we can even think about making a sale, we have to be someone who is worth following. And the way we become someone who is worth following is by building a solid foundation on social media, a foundation that will last.

So, how do we do this? We have to go back to our purpose for life—to glorify God—which drives every other purpose, including for being on social media. We have to start by having a clear vision of what our goals are for social media, and truthfully, this is a step many leaders overlook. If we just jump into social media without having a clear understanding of our why and our purpose for it, we'll end up spending a lot of time doing things that will not get us the results we were hoping for. When obstacles inevitably come, our frustrations can take over, and if we don't stay steady in our clear purpose, eventually we'll give up on social media.

From the time I was eighteen, I knew God had called me to full-time ministry. As I went through college and then on to seminary, God opened some incredible doors for me. While living in Texas I had the opportunity to fulfill my dream of working in youth ministry full-time, and God also allowed me to fulfill my dream of public speaking by allowing me to speak at several events. Things were looking great! I had my entire life ahead of me, and I knew God was going to use me in the church as a full-time ministry leader.

Unfortunately, that dream ended quickly as I felt multiple setbacks to those dreams. However, I still had this little nagging feeling inside of me. I still questioned why the dreams I had as an eighteen-year-old were not coming true. Why would God send me to seminary to then work in education? What happened to the speaking opportunities? What happened to the visions that God had given me?

Honestly, I lived with these questions for years. In 2011, I resigned from education to come home to be with my son and to finally go after the dreams that I felt God had placed in my life. I no longer wanted to work for someone else; I wanted to be an entrepreneur who changed lives.

Little did I know that God would lead me to social media. Little did I know that God would intertwine all of the hopes and dreams I had as an eighteen-year old and apply them to this new field. Little did I know that God was going to use me and the gifts He had given me, after all. Oh, how little I knew!

In my quest to find answers, to hear from God about why my life looked so different from the one I envisioned years ago, I came across some timeless truths that have encouraged my heart at times of despair, confusion, hurt, and anger. With eyes wide open and a heart longing for peace, I came to realize that God has always had my dreams in mind and that He is using them in ways I never imagined, in ways that are greater and bigger than what my little mind ever could have hoped for.

So this is where we start on our journey to social-media success. We start with some basic life lessons that will be the foundation for learning how to #BeWorthFollowing. Here are the truths I've learned that underlie everything we're going to discuss.

Trust God, even when you don't have all the answers.

"By an act of faith, Abraham said yes to God's call to travel to an unknown place that would become his home. When he left he had no idea where he was going. By an act of faith he lived in the country promised him, lived as a stranger camping in tents" (Hebrews 11:8 MSG). Let's say it again: God dreamers don't trust their own voices and ideas; instead, they trust the voice and ideas of God. So many times, God doesn't give us the full picture all at once. Instead, He gives us the dream and shows us the next step and simply wants us to obey. And once we obey, He then gives us a glimpse of what He has next for us. Clarity comes through the obedience.

Despite the hurt, confusion and anger I've felt through my ups and downs, God has been leading me all along, just as He's been leading you. Every experience I have been through has prepared me for where He has me right now. The dreams I had of being in ministry full-time, reaching people around the world, speaking and encouraging the hearts of women—He has brought about. In my role as a social-media/communication specialist, I have the opportunity to be a part of everything I dreamed of when I was in seminary. Every hurtful word that was spoken to me has prepared me for where I am right now. And I have to believe He is doing the same thing for you too.

He knows what we can handle in every season of life, because seasons change. Other realities and responsibilities and life lessons ebb and flow, and so does our work. Consider where you are in life and what God is saying to you today. Sink yourself into right now, with Him at the helm, no matter whether that strategy seems unconventional compared to what others are telling you about success.

Let God build your platform.

My pursuit of social media as a career started in 2012. I knew in order to gain expertise in the field and to be seen as a "specialist," I had to get likes and follows. I initially wondered, *How in the world am I going to get more people to follow me on Twitter and "like" me on Facebook?* I had no idea what I was doing. I just knew that my entire focus needed to be on increasing my numbers because I needed to be a legitimate expert in the field if I was going to be a social-media manager. I remember looking at all the other social-media gurus with their big numbers, asking, "Will I ever get there?"

As I learned how to navigate the world of social media, God showed me a way to gain a following that is outside of the current norm. A way that is not common talk amongst the social-media influencers.

> "Don't worry about building a platform. If you listen to God, people will listen to you because you will have something to say."
>
> ~Mark Batterson, *Draw the Circle: The 40 Day Prayer Challenge*1

I was taken back when I heard this at a social-media training: "See what's working for them and duplicate it." What this speaker was saying is that the best way to grow your numbers and expand your reach is to be a copycat. While it can be important to watch the experts, copying is not the best road to travel. Unfortunately, the thinking behind this is flawed. The emphasis is on copying and numbers, but there is *so much more* to social media than just the numbers.

Here is the hardcore truth: The impact you can make on social media has nothing to do with your numbers. There is no secret number that you need to attain before you are successful, before you can make a difference in someone's life.

Look at what *The Message* version of Romans 9:27 says:

If each grain of sand on the seashore were numbered and the sum labeled "chosen of God," They'd be numbers still, not names; salvation comes by personal selection. God doesn't count us; he calls us by name. Arithmetic is not his focus.

God is interested in people more than numbers. Sure, He cares about the whole population, but He also focuses on each person in the world. And He has certain people He wants to reach through you and your social-media presence. High or low numbers, that's not the top priority. How well we reach the ones He sends our way is what matters most.

Unfortunately, in our social-media-crazed world, all we hear about are the numbers: How many followers you have, how many likes a post got, how many comments you received, how many people retweeted your tweet, how many people are talking about your posts, what is your organic reach. Focusing on these items creates a tremendous amount of stress, and the emphasis is in the wrong place.

Does this mean we set social media to the side and do nothing because hey, God will write across the sky what we're supposed to post at what time? No. What it means is that once you start to focus on what's important and what matters, the other things will fall into place—specifically, your platform, your message and your numbers.

Take a deep breath and know that your numbers are not the measure of your effectiveness on social media. Your effectiveness is measured by the positive impact you're making. That's what social media is all about.

With a foundation based on pursuing God's dreams for you in order to primarily further His Kingdom purposes, and by letting Him build the platform, you'll be well fit to face the challenges.

"You don't have to seek opportunity. All you have to do is seek God. And if you seek God, opportunity will seek you."

~Mark Batterson, *Draw the Circle2*

Tips from the front line

Want to connect, engage and be successful on Twitter? Here are some pro tips:

- Don't be afraid to follow people. Many times Twitter requires that you take the first bold step in connecting with someone. Connect and then engage with their content. This opens the door for future engagement.

- If you are using Twitter for business, DO NOT, I repeat, DO NOT "protect" your tweets or make your Twitter profile private. The harder you make it for people to connect with you, the less people will connect with you.

- If you are going to use a prescheduled direct message (a message that automatically goes out to your new followers), do not make your message about you. Don't ask people to follow you on another platform. Don't try to get them to download your eBook or even worse, purchase your book, product or service. Instead, ask an intriguing question that 1) they will want to answer (make it about them) and 2) will help open the doors to future conversations.

- Be sure to follow people back. Nothing looks worse than having thousands of followers without following anyone back.

When you do that, it gives off the impression that you just don't care about the people who are following you.

- Be sure to use hashtags in your tweets when you can. It's been said that tweets that contain hashtags are more likely to get retweeted. Using the right hashtags helps you and your content get found.

- Post images with your tweets as often as you can. Again, research has shown that tweets with images get a much higher engagement rate.

- Try to keep your tweets short (since the limit is 280 characters). Why? Because you want to give people the opportunity to directly retweet your tweet, without having to change things up.

Check out the insights that Twitter offers you. You'll get insight that includes your engagement rate, what tweets got the most engagement, your top tweet, the number of retweets, likes and clicks your tweets have received and your top follower and mention.

Questions to consider

1. What do you need to ask God for help with?
2. What do you want to see God do for you? through you?
3. Right now, write down when you will have your "business meeting" with God each day. What time and where?
4. Will you ask God to help you entrust your numbers to Him, and ask Him to guide the building of your dream?

Tweetable moments

"Seek him with every fiber of your being, continue being faithful to Him & opportunity will seek YOU." ~@DrJenBennett, #BeWorthFollowing

"Maintaining a God-focus leads to the health of everything else in our lives, including our business and ministry." ~@DrJenBennett, #BeWorthFollowing

"There is SO MUCH MORE to social media than just the numbers." ~@DrJenBennett, #BeWorthFollowing

"Social media is about impacting the lives of others & your numbers have NOTHING to do with that impact" ~@DrJenBennett, #BeWorthFollowing

"Make your business or ministry about building the Kingdom...and watch how he brings opportunities your way to glorify him—and to provide for you and through you." ~@DrJenBennett, #BeWorthFollowing

"There is no secret # that you need to attain before you can impact the life of someone on social media." ~@DrJenBennett, #BeWorthFollowing

"Your effectiveness on social media is measured by the positive impact that you are making! ~@DrJenBennett, #BeWorthFollowing

"God-Sized Dreamers don't trust their own voice & ideas, they trust the voice & ideas of God." ~@DrJenBennett, #BeWorthFollowing

"Before we can even think about making a sale, we have to be someone who is worth following." ~@DrJenBennett, #BeWorthFollowing

"Clarity comes through the obedience." ~@DrJenBennett, #BeWorthFollowing

Chapter 3: #BeHealthy
Your Best You

Concentrate on doing your best for God, work you won't be ashamed of.

2 Timothy 2:15, MSG

Over the years as I've shared how to broaden our social-media scope, one question I get asked often is "Jen, what do I post? I have no idea where to begin or what I should put on social media." If you have found yourself asking this question, you are not alone.

Here's the quick-and-easy answer: Stop worrying about what to post and instead, work on building *you*. The more you get in tune with God and allow Him to mold and shape you, the more He's going to speak to you and give you the words to share with the world, words that bring value, hope, and inspiration.

If you want to build a social-media platform with an engaged community who is eager to chat with you, you have to be willing to work on who you are and your character. You have to know who you are and what you offer this world.

You also have to know what your hang-ups are, how they trigger negativity and resistance to forgiveness, and how they could hold you back if you don't proactively deal with them and let

God heal them. We've all got 'em, and we can't get past 'em till we own 'em. We need to claim our own baggage, then take it to God and check it with Him, accepting His forgiveness and healing in return. We also need to forgive others and ourselves for past hurts.

> "Pray as though everything depended on God. Work as though everything depended on you."
>
> ~Saint Augustine

As you work on you and your relationship with God, don't dismiss the fact that if you want to be taken seriously and have a successful business and ministry, you must also get good at what you do. Be willing to look hard at the things you need to work on inside, as well as get the training and experience you need. Also be willing to do whatever it takes to excel at your craft so that you can stand out and be the best in your industry. Be willing to do your part.

Focus on being the best version of yourself—and the other pieces of the puzzle will fall into place.

Get rid of the negative self-talk!

When I was younger, let's just say I was not the most popular girl. Elementary and part of middle school were tough, as they are for many kids. If the good Lord would somehow remove those years of growth and jump us right from being ten to being fifteen, maybe we'd all skip some pubescent angst! I'm kidding. We grow through adversity.

But back then I wasn't the skinniest girl and the kids noticed. I was called names that hurt. I never felt like I was pretty enough or skinny enough. I longed for the day when I could look like someone else.

It wasn't until eighth grade that I actually started to like myself a little. The baby fat started going away and boys started noticing me. Finally, I was a happy girl.

But soon into high school, I had another demon to deal with. I didn't feel smart enough. I failed geometry and because of that, I was relegated to the "stupid" math class (at least that's what it was known as in high school). Honestly, I just wanted to get out of high school. It wasn't my thing.

When I got to college I started to like school and realized that I did have a brain. Math wasn't my strong suit (I chose a statistics math class with a teacher who was known to give easy As), but I soon began to realize that I had strengths in other areas. I got involved on campus and became the president of a variety of on-campus organizations. I was a resident assistant who won the RA of the year award, and I was on homecoming court. Things were going great.

But we all keep a bit of the struggling adolescent tucked inside of ourselves, no matter how old and accomplished we may become. It keeps us humble, which can actually be to our benefit if we've dealt with our hurts and view them in a healthy way.

Yet life has a way of bringing tough memories and insecurities back around to haunt us during challenging times like building a business or dealing with negative online feedback, and we need to reset our convictions and sureness of God's dreams for us and his strength within us.

Although I found my niches in college and was thriving, I still had some of those nagging thoughts from childhood that would try to get the best of me. You know, thoughts like:

- You're not pretty enough.
- You're not skinny enough.
- You're not fashionable enough.
- You're not smart enough.

And later as I began venturing out into the world of entrepreneurship, other thoughts entered and flooded my mind:

- You don't have the money.
- You don't have the skills.
- You don't have the right connections.
- You don't have the right look.
- You don't have the right training.
- You're not like so and so.
- You don't have the big following.
- You don't have the *right* numbers.

All negative self-talk! Self-talk that was trying to bring me down and keep me from fulfilling the call that God had on my life. And you know what? Sometimes I think it's the negative self-talk that holds us back more than the hurts of the past. Often, we become our worst enemies.

Think about it. For many of us, if anyone spoke to us (or our kids) the way that we speak to ourselves on a daily basis, we would remove them from our lives. We would no longer communicate with them. So why do we do this to ourselves? Why do we sabotage what is possible for us by demeaning ourselves with the words we speak?

What we say to ourselves is a reflection of our heart and what we really believe about ourselves. And the hard-core truth is, your words to yourself will either move you forward or hold you back.

Your words to yourself will either move you forward or hold you back.

As long as you continue to focus on what you think are your inadequacies, you won't find the success you're seeking. You will never move forward into the glorious calling that God has given you as long as you continue to tell yourself what you lack and what you think you can't do. Your words give you life, and it can be a life filled with risk and adventure or a life filled with doubts, regrets and lost dreams.

What beliefs about yourself are you holding today? What beliefs are causing you to speak badly to yourself? See if any of the following self-criticisms sound familiar:

- I'm not that creative.
- I don't have the money.
- I don't have the time.
- I'm not that smart.
- I don't have a college degree.
- I'm too introverted to succeed.
- I don't know the right people.
- I'm not good enough.
- What I do isn't important.
- What I do doesn't really matter.
- What I do isn't making a difference.
- I'm too old.
- I'm too young.
- I don't have experience.
- I don't have what it takes.
- I'm a slow learner.

If you want to succeed in business, ministry, social media and in life, you have to get rid of the negative self-talk, the limiting beliefs that are holding you back. As long as you continue to believe these things and talk to yourself in this manner, you will not experience abundant living.

Speak truth into your heart from God's Word. Satan, the enemy of God's followers, takes special notice of those whose lives are centered on God's priorities. But we have an arsenal of truth to fight back with the Holy Spirit's power. Disciplining ourselves with regular input of what's true and right and admirable and praiseworthy will steady us and fight the lies. Try out some of these truths:

- I'd say you'll do best by filling your minds and meditating on things true, noble, reputable, authentic, compelling, gracious—the best, not the worst; the beautiful, not the ugly; things to praise, not things to curse. Put into practice what you learned from me, what you heard and saw and realized. Do that, and God, who makes everything work together, will work you into his most excellent harmonies. Philippians 4:8–9, MSG

- This means that anyone who belongs to Christ has become a new person. The old life is gone; a new life has begun! 2 Corinthians 5:17, NLT

- Whatever I have, wherever I am, I can make it through anything in the One who makes me who I am. Philippians 4:13, MSG

- "If you stick with this, living out what I tell you, you are my disciples for sure. Then you will experience for yourselves the truth, and the truth will free you." John 8:31–32, NLT

- In Christ lives all the fullness of God in a human body. So you also are complete through your union with Christ, who is the head over every ruler and authority. Colossians 2:9–10, NLT

- There has never been the slightest doubt in my mind that the God who started this great work in you would keep at it and bring it to a flourishing finish on the very day Christ Jesus appears. Philippians 1:6, MSG

- So let's not allow ourselves to get fatigued doing good. At the right time we will harvest a good crop if we don't give up, or quit. Right now, therefore, every time we get the chance, let us work for the benefit of all, starting with the people closest to us in the community of faith. Galatians 6:9, MSG

- For we are his workmanship, created in Christ Jesus for good works, which God prepared beforehand, that we should walk in them. Ephesians 2:10, ESV

Choose to forgive.

There will come a point where you have to give over your hurts, bitterness, anger, regrets, questions, worries, anxiety and confusion. If you want to experience what God has next for you, you are going to have to let go of the negativity from the past. Let it all go!

If you want to be successful on social media, in your business, and in life, you have to be willing to forgive, and you have to be willing to let go of all the junk that has been holding you back for far too long.

Why is forgiveness so important? How could holding on to hurts and grudges hold us back? Well, you may have heard that we forgive not so much for the other person, but really in order to set ourselves free. Unforgiveness is toxic to our systems. When we harbor it in our hearts, it creates an atmosphere for all kinds of other attitudes that sour our outlook on life and our view of our place in it. It's hard to process things in a healthy way when unforgiveness is darkening our spirit.

In order to experience success in all areas of your life (including social media), it's vitally important that you not only forgive those who have hurt you, but that you also forgive yourself. As long as you are leaving room for bitterness and talking down to yourself, you will never reach the success that you are capable of reaching. That is why forgiveness must be among the first things we tackle on this journey. I want you to experience all that God has for you. I want to see you living a life you love, and growing a business that is impacting many lives. I want your social-media platform to *rock*.

Don't toy with comparison.

Comparing ourselves with others, a slippery slope if there ever was one! Toying with it is a surefire way to manufacture trouble for ourselves, and common sense has to ask, Why in the world would we do that?

A little comparison goes a long way to create a habit of ungratefulness, an attitude of dissatisfaction, and pattern of envy and even judgmentalism. Like perfectionism and jealousy, comparison creates an environment where you can never keep up or measure up or truly be happy for someone else's success. And it robs the fullness of joy from our own successes. We've got to take charge on this one, friends, and cast off every comparing thought that crosses our minds.

Take responsibility for doing the creative best you can with your own life.

Galatians 6:5, MSG

Think about the last time you compared yourself with someone, or your business or ministry with another's. Somehow it ended up badly, right? Either you ended up feeling like you aren't doing enough or aren't worthy enough. Or possibly that they must be pleasing God more, or on the other hand (gasp) not living for him enough since they don't seem to be faced with spiritual challenges in their work.

None of these responses is healthy or godly. While there is nothing wrong with learning from observing how others utilize social media, we have to keep our eyes, minds, and hearts disciplined to shut off Facebook if it appears everyone else is living the dream while ours feels as if it's asthmatic.

We'll talk more about being real later, but for now, let's be real with ourselves and admit that most of us put our most bright and shining faces on social media, despite the fact that no one has it all together. All are wounded. All of us are easy targets for the comparison trap. So let's not toy with it.

God has a unique plan for each of us, for our work and ministry efforts. Focusing on Him and what He wants to do in and through us will be our stabilizing force that assures us we don't need to compare ourselves to anyone else.

No victim mentality around here! No saying that if you were like such and such, your life would look different. Take responsibility for your life. Do the creative best that you can do. Utilize what God has given you and see Him move.

Don't be afraid.

So go ahead, don't be afraid to be you. We are going to discuss in detail how to do that, throughout this book. Don't be afraid to start taking joy in your strengths and all that you have to offer this world. Don't be afraid to be the healthy you that you were created to be!

> *For we are God's handiwork, created in Christ Jesus to do good works, which God prepared in advance for us to do.*
> *~Ephesians 2:10, NIV*

Tips from the front line

Instagram is a great platform that allows you to share the visual story of your business/ministry and life. It has quickly become one of the top platforms, so here are some tips to help you get started:

- Fill out your profile completely. Share some of the main points about who you and what your business/ministry is. Make sure you include a great-looking profile picture.
- If you will be using Instagram for business, then use a business profile. Having a business profile on IG gives you a "Contact" button that allows visitors to your profile to email you, call you

or get directions to your location. Additionally with a business profile, you get access to some analytics that include impressions, reach, profile views and website clicks. You can even get insights on individual posts.

Also, with a business account, you can take advantage of promoting a post that will allow you to either have people visit your website or call/visit your business. Much like Facebook ads, you can create your own audience to target your post to, choose a budget, and decide how long you want your promotion to run for. You can also choose an "action button," which is basically a call to action that includes, "learn more," "watch more," "shop now," "book now," "sign up," or "contact us."

Questions to consider

Take some time to dig deeply into your thoughts. Grab your journal, favorite pen and favorite drink and work through these questions. I promise, the more time you spend getting to know yourself, the better prepared you will be to succeed in life and in business.

1. What hurts are you still holding on to?
2. What lies from others are you still believing?
3. What words are you speaking to yourself on a daily basis?
4. How are you currently working on YOU?
5. Where do you feel under qualified?
6. Who in your life breathes life into you?
7. What are you ready to let go of today?

Tweetable moments

"Why do we sabotage what is possible for us by demeaning ourselves with the words we speak?" ~@DrJenBennett, #BeWorthFollowing

"What we say to ourselves is a reflection of our heart & what it is that we believe about ourselves." ~@DrJenBennett, #BeWorthFollowing

"The hard-core truth is, your words to yourself will either move you forward or hold you back." ~~@DrJenBennett, #BeWorthFollowing

"You'll never move forward into your God calling as long as you tell yourself what you lack." ~@DrJenBennett, #BeWorthFollowing

"Your words will give you a life filled w/adventure or a life filled w/doubts, regrets & lost dreams." ~@DrJenBennett, #BeWorthFollowing

"If you want to succeed in biz, social media & life, get rid of the limiting beliefs that hold you back." ~@DrJenBennett, #BeWorthFollowing

"Don't be afraid to start taking joy in your strengths and all that you have to offer this world." ~@DrJenBennett, #BeWorthFollowing

"Stop worrying about what to post and instead, work on building YOU!" ~@DrJenBennett, #BeWorthFollowing

Chapter 4: #BeGiving
Don't Sell—Serve

● ● ● ● ● ● ●

Give away your life; you'll find life given back, but not merely given back—given back with bonus and blessing. Giving, not getting, is the way.

Luke 6:38, MSG

So far we've established that our focus on God needs to come first, and we need to work on our own character. A natural outflow of those priorities leads to a heart attitude of generosity that wants the best for others. This combination is key; it makes the difference as to how we come across to our customers and colleagues. When others can see that we are not trying to get them to do something to benefit us—meaning selling, selling, selling—they will be drawn to appreciate and trust us enough to do business with us.

Author Jay Baer has it right. In his book, *Youtility* (which I highly recommend), he says, "Stop trying to be amazing and start being useful."[3] Of course, we have to do our jobs with excellence, making sure our skills are honed to offer the best quality. But what speaks every bit as loudly is our desire to serve.

Often, our attempts at platform building focus on selling. Our posts target potential clients or buyers with sales pitches. We talk incessantly about our products and services—because that's how we make our money, and we think people need to know all about what we offer.

But we need to shift our thinking. God gifted us with our skills and talents so that we can use them to serve others. What if we develop our business platforms in that context? In order to truly make a difference, our platforms should showcase our character, how we build relationships, and how we can provide people with something they want or need.

Often, what we want are viral posts. Viral posts make sense in a world where viral equals famous. We're surrounded by viral news, viral videos, and viral everything. We spend time seeking high numbers by doing what the experts are doing. After all, their posts go viral. We want our posts to go viral too.

But maybe viral posts are the result of the solid foundation we're laying. A foundation that includes being useful, serving others, and being different. The numbers will naturally come because you will stand out among a noisy social-media world. The noise comes from all of the experts and non-experts attempting to get numbers for the sake of numbers, attempting to be amazing without substance, and creating themselves as carbon copies of someone else. We need to stand out by doing something other than adding to the noise. We need to be useful. We need to #BeWorthFollowing.

Be unselfish and others-oriented.

In social media, as in life, if we are merely trying to toot our own horn, our customers can tell. When we just want them to sign on the dotted line and add to our numbers, they are turned off, and for good reason.

People can tell when they are being used for someone else's benefit. Sure, we are selling something, trying to make a living; but our attitude toward that end is essential. If our heart attitude is really to give something of value to someone else, our unselfishness shows, just as the flip side is true. We're willing to go the extra mile because it is the right thing to do, for someone else's good. We're willing to engage with others to get to know them, not for them to see how brightly we can shine or how many other people like us.

> *Don't be selfish; don't try to impress others. Be humble, thinking of others as better than yourselves. Don't look out only for your own interests, but take an interest in others, too.*
>
> *Philippians 2:3–4, NLT*

This focus on unselfishness might seem obvious or unnecessary to point out, but it bears repeating to ourselves on a regular basis. We humans were not created to be glorified. That premier role is God's, and He is the only one who can handle it well 24/7 over the test of time.

A wise person once said that we were not made for fame. Does that mean being famous is wrong? Of course not. But consider all of the reality stars and even plenty of big-name spiritual leaders over the past decade or two who have "fallen from grace," as it's said. Particularly when a believer is working to promote the Gospel, we become targets for the enemy, who hates Jesus, salvation, and all Jesus' followers—but loves to use our human weaknesses, our basic human desire to matter and to be influential, to our downfall and to seek to diminish the message of Jesus in this world. There is a lot at stake when Christians pursue large audiences, and the repercussions can be weighty.

Desiring to be in the limelight, to have lots of followers, ought to be thoroughly thought through, because it comes with great responsibility to live well for Christ and to promote His name more than our own.

Even so, God has given us the role to lift Him up and live for Him publicly in this world, so we must move ahead with this charge! The dreams He has given us are ones through which He intends to fulfill His eternal plans.

That's big, big stuff! And we are invited to be part in it, unselfishly.

One key to being someone who is worth following on social media is to give more than you expect to get. And by serving and helping people, you will stand out from the noise for the right reasons.

Consider this guy.

You may know the story of the Good Samaritan (see Luke 10:25–37). He was a normal guy who was living his life, walking along the road one day when he passed another man (who wasn't even in his tribe) who was horribly wounded.

The Samaritan could have been like the two leaders who had already walked on and left the man in need. But this Samaritan was others-oriented. He was not self-important, basking in his own position, pursuing his own good first, as the two leaders were.

He cared for the man by taking him to a hotel and seeing to his needs.

His story did not make it into the Bible because he was known as a catchy speaker or he had a fabulous product to sell or he was looked up to for his many opinions or pithy humor or trendy image.

Neither did his story make it into God's Word because he worked his tail off to promote the grand thing he'd done.

His story made it into God's eternal Word because of his rare and timely unselfishness.

He was not living to make a name for himself or to draw attention to his platform.

He simply served as needed.

Yet we still read of him today because God wanted to touch others—ourselves included—through this man's daily life. His simple act of giving made much of *God's* platform.

Imagine that.

Now imagine God doing similar things (for now and eternity) through you and me. We may be *marketing* our ministry or business, but make no mistake, as believers we are *promoting* God's Kingdom. Whether we promote it with all our hearts, souls, bodies, and minds is up to us as far as how hard we are willing to work, balancing our work with priorities of serving family and those in our immediate (offline) circle—not to mention healthy rest.

Let's not add to the online noise. There's too much of that already.

Instead, when you focus on what's important and what really matters, your platforms and message will fall into place. The numbers will come as God fulfills His purposes through your efforts.

Tips from the front line

Do you know what keywords are? Believe it or not, keywords are vitally important to your online influence. Keywords are basically the words and phrases that people use when searching for something specific on the Internet. Things like:

- Open houses this weekend in Orlando, Florida
- Books about social media
- How do I find a literary agent?

"Keywords" tend to be short phrases that people search for. And based on the keywords that leaders use on their websites, blog posts, social-media platforms, etc., allow them to be "found" when people are searching for what they have to offer.

One of the best things you can do for your business/ministry is to know the top 5–10 keywords and keyword phrases your target audience uses. Knowing this will allow you to be found online.

While there are many "tools" out there that will help you find your top keywords, I recommend using Google Keyword Planner when you are getting started. This tool is a free AdWords tool that allows you to search for those keywords that your audience is using when searching for what you have online. Know that when you go to research and use Google Keyword planner, you will b required to set-up an AdWords account, but you never have to use it for paid advertising.

Once you start researching keywords, look for those that have both high and low average monthly searches. And know that those that have high monthly searches, mean that they are more competitive which in turn, will make it a bit harder for you to be found on Google (for example, the keywords: Social Media Marketing).

As you conduct your research, be sure to write down every possible Keyword and Keyword phrase that could work for you. And then always keep that list handy.

Questions to consider

1. When has someone's unselfishness blessed you?
2. Could your focus toward serving be better each day?
3. What online noise has turned you off lately? Why?
4. How might your posts and responses be impacted with more of an others-orientation?
5. How might your entire attitude toward your business/ministry change by shifting the pressure from gaining numbers to serving others?
6. Do you trust God enough to take care of the numbers He knows you need, as you maintain the primary focus He wants you to have? Pray over this and ask Him to grow your faith! A courageous prayer but one He loves to answer.

Tweetable moments

"When you focus on what's important & what really matters, your platforms & message will fall into place." ~@DrJenBennett, #BeWorthFollowing

"We may be *marketing* our ministry or business, but make no mistake, as believers we are *promoting* God's Kingdom."
~@DrJenBennett, #BeWorthFollowing

"God has given us the role to lift Him up and live for him publicly in this world, so we must move ahead with this charge!"
~@DrJenBennett, #BeWorthFollowing

"One key to being someone who is worth following on social media is to give more than you expect to get."
~@DrJenBennett, #BeWorthFollowing

"By serving and helping people, you will stand out from the noise for the right reasons." ~@DrJenBennett, #BeWorthFollowing

"Desiring to be in the limelight, to have lots of followers ... comes with great responsibility to live well for Christ and to promote His name more than our own." ~@DrJenBennett, #BeWorthFollowing

"Maybe viral posts are the result of a solid foundation ... that includes being useful, serving others, and being different."
~@DrJenBennett, #BeWorthFollowing

"The numbers will naturally come because you will stand out among a noisy social-media world." ~@DrJenBennett, #BeWorthFollowing

Part II: Building Blocks

● ● ● ● ● ● ●

How do we build on the foundation of pointing our focus toward God, trusting that He gives us our identity and knows how He wants to use us? How do we know that we know who we are and what our unique purpose is? Through knowing whose we are. We get our purpose, our action plan, our mission statement from Him. In that light …

Chapter 5: #BeDifferent
Uniquely You: What's Your Point?

God is working in you, giving you the desire and the power to do what pleases him.

Philippians 2:13, NLT

Don't let comparison cripple the real you.

We've talked about comparison. Now let's think through some of the online triggers that can trap us into comparing ourselves with others. Spend a few minutes scrolling through the newsfeed on Facebook (or any social-media platform) and within a matter of seconds you'll find yourself inundated with stories. Stories like:

- the birth and celebration of a new baby
- the engagement of two souls
- the business success of an entrepreneurial friend
- friends purchasing a new home or new car
- your competitor making $5000 in less than two hours

You see friends enjoying a date night with their spouse, friends on the vacation of a lifetime, friends who just landed that dream job they've been praying about, friends enjoying a girls' weekend at a spiffy resort, your competitor receiving another speaking engagement request. While seeing all of these stories, you can't help but think:

- The last date night I had with my husband was when we were dating.
- I wish I had money for a vacation.
- I hate my job and if I could quit today, I would—but I have too much debt.
- Girls' weekend getaway? I wish I had the time, the money, and the friends!
- I've been working my business for three years, and I'm lucky if I can make $5,000 in six months.

The list goes on and sounds familiar, right? After a while, you walk away from the Internet feeling sad, depressed, overwhelmed, and anxious. Eventually, you start wondering why your life isn't filled with all of these *glamorous* moments. All of a sudden, you realize, *This isn't the life I signed up for and (worse!) it's boring.*

Once you've read all the good news, comparisons are inevitable. How can you possibly measure up? How do all those people look so camera ready in every picture? Don't they ever wear sweats or skip lipstick or have a bad hair day? Oh wait, there's a woman in sweats—but she looks incredible!

And then there's the mom stuff. One friend just helped her kids make extravagant Valentine's boxes for their school parties (next thing you know, they'll be putting motors on those!). Or someone else posts their indoor/outdoor Christmas decorations the day after Thanksgiving, but you feel lucky each year to eke out time to finish gift shopping by midnight on Christmas Eve. You think your Christmas ornaments look old and not in the good way, your "homemade" cookies came from a refrigerator tube, and stringing lights outside—when? You hate baking and there is not one crafty bone in you. Not only that, but your kid didn't get the second-grade math award at school like that other mom's child did, and it's entirely because you don't understand the new math, and no doubt it will affect his college possibilities. AND your house's Tooth Fairy ought to be fired for delinquency! What lousy fairy-tale gig is she running? (I really hope you're laughing now.)

Or, on the work front, you see your competitor having great success with a recent product launch, and you start going crazy with ideas of how you too can make the same exact product so that you can experience success and cash flow. "Why didn't I think of it first?" you chastise yourself.

How do I know all of this? Because I too have struggled with comparisons and beating myself up over all the ways I haven't seemed to cut it—even when it's my own misperceptions. I've walked away from the computer feeling like my life doesn't measure up. I've walked away wondering if I'm a good mommy. I've walked away feeling like something was wrong with me because I wasn't experiencing the success my competitor was having. And, I've walked away wondering why my life couldn't look different.

When I first started out in social media, I consistently looked at the platforms of my competitors. I watched what they were doing, who was following them, and what they were posting. The more I *watched them* the more I became dissatisfied in what I was doing, offering and promoting. The more time I spent looking at their platforms, the more I felt as though I couldn't succeed, I couldn't be used by God. And, even though I hate to admit this, the more I watched their platforms, the angrier I became. I just couldn't understand why they were experiencing so much success as my platforms were sputtering. It didn't seem fair.

I found myself in a slump. I questioned what God was doing in my life and in my business. I spent so much time comparing that I failed to see the story that God wanted to share through me.

I didn't see the unique voice, skills and talents He had given me. I couldn't see how God would use my uniqueness to reach an audience that He would bring to me. I had allowed the sin of envy to enter into my life, and I had to deal with it.

You see, comparison and envy will kill our dreams.

Envy will keep you from following the calling of God on your life. The time you spend comparing and envying what someone else has will only hold you back and weaken the beautiful work God wants to do through you—and it will be beautiful if you let go and let Him lead.

Where does it end? Is it possible to enjoy social media without allowing our thoughts to lead us astray?

How can you break away from this trap? How can you continue moving forward on your unique path, even when you see all of these things taking place on social media? To help you move past the comparison trap and to be someone worth following (no whiny posts, no arguments, no negativity), here are some tips that help me not only enjoy social media, but also help me to avoid the ugliness that can so easily overtake the online world. Let's go back to Galatians 6. I believe it has the answer for us:

Make a careful exploration of who you are and the work you have been given, and then sink yourself into that. Don't be impressed with yourself. Don't compare yourself with others. Each of you must take responsibility for doing the creative best you can with your own life. ~Galatians 6:4–5, MSG

When we compare, we lose sight of our real selves, and we cheat ourselves from the blessing of living in the wholeness of God's love for us. We can't be our best selves unless we are our real selves.

What makes you YOU?

Being the real you leads to being your best you. Do you believe that? It might sound odd, or not humble, but consider making a list of your strengths. Those come in various forms, including innate talents, skills you've learned, character strengths, life experiences, schooling or other training, spiritual gifts, and personality traits. This is not an arrogant project; it's a healthy one. So go ahead and remind yourself of your best!

Maybe you are industrious and you love a new project. Maybe you love to organize or you're always thinking of the details, or you're one to reach out to someone who is hurting. Maybe you are able to speak or write with rare compassion and truth. Maybe your business savvy has always been something you've felt good about but have never officially acknowledged to yourself. It's important to include qualities on your list that make up who you are, not just what you've done. Both have value.

Go ahead and write them down, even (especially) the little things. Don't rush. Do this over several days or a week, allowing new realizations to come to you as you take a (probably) rare inventory of all the positives that make you unique. Call them what they are. Write them down. Make it official. You are a unique masterpiece!

Looking over your list, do you see the treasure God created in you? No one else has ever been exactly like you; therefore, no one else can be the you God wants to use for His good purposes.

Does reading the list give you a sense of awe? Self-consciousness? Gratitude? New motivation? Maybe it makes you wonder why it's so much easier to fall into a trap of comparing ourselves to others than it is to fully appreciate the way our Maker made each of us one-of-a-kind.

What if we noticed all those enviable stories mentioned in the previous section, in light of our "asset" list we've compiled. We're armed with the truth! Imagine the benefits of casting off comparison and making the most of our own wonderful unique-nesses. Is that possible?

Yes! But we have to reach a point in our lives where we are grateful for all that God has done. We have to see and realize the unique skills and talents that He has given us.

1. **Review your careful exploration of who you are:** Keep your list of positive "you" qualities handy. Get comfortable with these questions: Do you know who you are? Do you know how God has uniquely created you? Do you know the gifts, skills and talents that He has given you? One of the ways to avoid the comparison trap is to take time to study yourself. Stop studying your competitor and instead, study who God made you to be.

2. **Commit to the work you have been given:** What season of life are you in right now? What work has God given you right now to complete? How can you use your gifts, skills and talents with the work that He has given you right now? Make a careful exploration of your work.

3. **Sink yourself into that:** Once you know who you are and the work that God has given you during this season of life, sink yourself into that. Stop wishing for better days. Stop wishing your life or business looked like that of your competitor. Instead, focus on the here and now and where God has you.

4. **Don't be impressed with yourself:** Once you start sinking yourself into your work and using the gifts, skills and talents that God has given you, doors will open. You will see God move. But don't get too impressed with yourself. Remember, God brought you here. Your main purpose is to love others, serve others and bring glory to God. It's all because of Him.

5. **Don't compare yourself with others:** Let God do what He wants to do in the lives of others, and let Him do what He wants to do in your life. He has a different assignment and calling for you! Stop trying to be like someone else. Follow the unique path He has given you.

6. **Embrace gratitude:** One of the best ways to overcome the tendency to compare our lives with those online is to keep a gratitude journal, and there are multiple ways to do this online. Make a commitment to add a few things that you are grateful for each day (not just during the month of November). You can create a document on Facebook, you can create a board on Pinterest, you can upload a picture each day on Instagram, you can even tweet your gratitude. Kick comparison, envy, jealousy, and discontent to the curb by focusing on what's going well.

How about a look at the story of a woman from long ago? It's told in Joshua 2. Rahab was not a person anyone would have singled out for success or to #BeWorthFollowing. She was a prostitute in the city of Jericho who had much going against her. Society viewed her as unworthy. She was an untrusted outcast. But she acted in faith on behalf of God's people to save them. She showed courage, sureness of her need for the one true God, and God created a beautiful legacy through her. She is in Jesus' ancestral line.

She was different. She was an unlikely success story, despite her past failures. And she lived for Someone bigger than herself. It was through her willingness to #BeDifferent and to #BeFaithful and to #BeFearless that we read of her efforts to save a nation.

Like Rahab, we need to #BeDifferent.

Develop your voice.

Another unique quality that sets you apart is your voice, the way you "sound" online. The more you share on your social-media platform(s), the more you'll come to recognize your signature voice.

If you follow me on social media, I trust you've observed that one of the characteristics I work hard for in my own social-media presence is a trademark upbeat, encouraging voice. I hope followers have come to expect no sarcasm, no politics or other hot-button social issues. Avoiding those topics doesn't equate with a lack of care about those things. But those aspects of life are not why my business exists online; instead, I aim to glorify God by empowering women to embrace their calling while making the most of social media to build their businesses and ministries.

With every post, my goal is that my voice will match my brand, logo, and online look—on the website and various platform pages.

Likewise, your voice ought to be recognizable and consistent with your purpose.

Consider these social-media leaders, Christian and secular. What are they known for? Here's a start; you may have other ideas:

- Ann Voskamp: thoughtful, spiritual depth, gratitude, healing from brokenness, lyrical voice
- Melanie Shankle (*Nobody's Cuter Than You*): humor, self-effacing, every woman's friend
- Ree Drummond (the Pioneer Woman): friendliness, cheerfulness, warmth
- Rachel Held Evans: frankness, focusing on the emergent church and social issues
- Beth Moore: humorous, passionate, Bible-focused teaching
- Christine Caine: exhortation
- Joanna Gaines: peaceful, unflappable, patient, encouraging
- Savannah Guthrie: perky, positive, approachable
- Kathie Lee Gifford: outspoken, outgoing, sociable, warm, goofy

These women come from all walks of life. Each one has a unique job and her own style and voice. Each one shines in her own way and reaches a whole lot of people, whether those people agree with everything they say or not. One thing they all have in common is their consistent voice. They come across like they know who they are. Sure, we know enough of human nature to assume they probably all have areas of insecurity too, just like the rest of us. But the point is, they balance their purpose and their voice effectively.

By developing your voice, you can #BeDifferent. Yours will not be like theirs, so no need to mimic. But no one else's will be quite like yours either, so own your specialness!

The key to determining your voice is figuring out what kind of personality your social-media presence will have.

Would it be:
✓ Formal
✓ Informal
✓ Inspirational
✓ Laid Back
✓ Humorous
✓ Warm
✓ Fun
✓ Simple
✓ Direct
✓ Community Driven
✓ Inviting
✓ Hip
✓ Playful
✓ Educational?

God wants to use you in a unique way, including making something beautiful from all the pieces of you, from your voice and your knowledge, your skills and experiences, and even your former mistakes and missteps. Don't compare yourself to everyone else on social media, and you won't miss out on His unique calling on *your* life.

Like kids are taught early on in elementary school: Be you. The world is waiting.

Tips from the front line

If you're a blogger, this one's for you! Blogging can be fun and challenging and a great way to invite people into your business or ministry world. But it's good to know a few things to make the most of it and avoid getting lost in Bloggerdom:

- Know your goal for blogging. What results do you hope to achieve?
- What will the focus be on your blogs? You don't want to confuse your readers, so make sure you have a specific focus for your writing topics.
- Do you know what the keywords are for your niche? Keywords help you get found on the Internet.
- Make your blogs easy to read. Provide some copy that is bold and provide bullet points. This helps break up the copy for those who are just scanning (which are the majority of people).
- Always include a featured image with your blog and make sure that the image goes along with the topic of your blog.
- Create an intriguing/inviting headline. Your headline will either cause people to stop and read or move on.
- Include social-media share buttons at the bottom of your blog. Give people the opportunity to share your writings on their platforms.
- NEVER require people to enter in a ton of information (like captcha codes) prior to leaving a comment on your blog.

Remember, you want to make it easy for them to comment and share with you.

- Share your blogs on your social-media platforms on a regular basis. And advertise those blog posts to your target audience so that you can get more eyes on them.

Questions to consider

1. What are your gifts, skills and talents? What do people always compliment you on?
2. How are you different from the competition? How do you and will you stand out?
3. What are your greatest strengths, skills and talents? Write them down and commit to focusing on these things.

Tweetable moments

"Don't let comparison cripple the real you." ~@DrJenBennett, #BeWorthFollowing

"Envy will keep you from following the calling of God on your life." ~@DrJenBennett, #BeWorthFollowing

"Stop studying your competitor and instead, study who you are!" ~@DrJenBennett, #BeWorthFollowing

"Stop trying to be like someone else. Follow the unique & different path that God has given you!" ~@DrJenBennett, #BeWorthFollowing

"Your voice ought to be recognizable and consistent with your purpose." ~@DrJenBennett, #BeWorthFollowing

"God wants to use you in a unique way, including making something beautiful from all the pieces of you." ~@DrJenBennett, #BeWorthFollowing

"Don't compare yourself to everyone else on social media, and you won't miss out on His unique calling on *your* life." ~@DrJenBennett, #BeWorthFollowing

Chapter 6: #BeReal
Let the True You Shine Through

The aim of our charge is love that issues from a pure heart and a good conscience and a sincere faith.

1 Timothy 1:5, ESV

People want to get to know you.

You can be an online leader who breaks the norm and doesn't create a picture-perfect image of yourself. By sharing your foibles and life's funnies, and by giving your tribe nuggets of the real you, people will learn to see that you are the honest-to-goodness deal behind the company logo or squeaky-clean ministry brand.

People want to be able to trust your business or ministry, but they need to know the person behind the brand in order to develop that faith in you. With trust, numbers naturally increase, partly because of word of mouth—the best marketing tool you can get. Word of mouth that comes from a time-tested reputation helps build a platform when you aren't even looking or directly doing the work.

We will discuss how to keep up a consistent and enduring trust later on. For now, I want to discuss how showing your audience who you really are can lay the foundation for trust to grow.

I've learned this over the years as I've opened up my imperfect life on social media. I haven't done this foolishly; sharing ourselves, especially online and with strangers, deserves careful thought and discernment. Too much information is not wise or wanted. But a peek into who we are behind the screen makes people feel a connection with us. And people crave connection of all kinds, in person and online.

Here are a few ways I shared myself that garnered great responses, which I in turn replied to, continuing to build on the personal side of my online presence.

One day, I really messed up. I had just finished having my mammogram and *the girls* were hurting! So, I decided to text my husband to let him know all was clear but that I was hurting. Well, this happened instead:

Jennifer Bennett
December 16, 2013 · Clermont, FL · 🌐 ▾

That akward moment when you text your husband telling him about your mammogram appointment and how your "-----" hurt, and after hitting send you realize you just texted your son's teacher. #TheStoryofMyLife #Classic #KeepingItReal

Like · Comment · Share · Buffer · 👍 76 💬 63

Yep, you read that right. Instead of texting my husband, I texted my son's teacher! I was so embarrassed.

And how about this very REAL shot of me during one of my Crossfit workouts. Yeah, not so glamorous!

Why am I sharing these crazy stories with you? Because they matter. We spend so much time trying to paint the picture-perfect life on social media, trying to craft the perfect posts, the glamorous pictures and the winning opportunities, that we fail to connect with our audience on a deeper level, a real level.

Your audience wants to know that they are not alone, that you have embarrassing moments too, that you don't always look perfect. And even that you experience hurts in life.

Like I said, you don't have to share everything online—and you shouldn't. Be choosy about what you will and will not share. But every post should not be picture perfect. People want to get to know the real you, so the key is to find the balance between "real" and "TMI."

Some stories like these draw laughter or smiles, but other times our news shows our real side by tugging at the heart. A while back, my son had a twenty-day fever. Yep, you read that right, a twenty-day fever that put him in the hospital with visits from multiple doctors. I was worried, tired, and at times, wondering where God was:

Jennifer Bennett
May 20, 2014 · 🌐 ▾

Well, tomorrow we head into day #12 of Liam having a fever. Still praying and asking God to make this nasty virus go away. Thursday we meet with another doctor to make sure nothing is being missed. Would love your continued prayers. This is emotionally draining for this momma......

Like · Comment · Share · Buffer · 👍 58 💬 50

And I'll never forget the time that I shared with my audience about my miscarriage: The outpouring I received blew me away. To know that people were praying on my behalf touched me in a way I never imagined. And I found hope in the messages of women who had gone through a miscarriage and were finding healing.

Your honest posts that share true struggles allow people to get a glimpse of the real you. When we spend too much time trying to compose posts that portray "perfection" in our lives and businesses (so that we can feel good about ourselves), we miss out on connecting with our audience. Most people can't relate to perfection (or live up to it, which is automatically discouraging)—but they can relate to bad days, dumb mistakes, and heartbreak. People can't connect with fake and don't want to; so instead, give them real.

So to the fitness guru whose posts showed impossible-to-live-up-to portrayals of the perfect, fit body, I recommended she share a picture of the time she wasn't all made up, looking great in her workout gear. To a professional organizer, I might recommend that she incorporate a fun "True Tuesday" post and show a weekly picture of a messy area in her home, office, or vehicle. Sometimes our best "real" posts are born through our messy human moments.

My challenge for you: Try to share at least three real moments online this week, whether they're stories or images. Let people into your world. Let people know the real you. Let people know you're human. Tell them your stories. #BeDifferent #BeWorthFollowing

Get to know the art of social-media storytelling.

For a moment, think back to your childhood. Do you remember the fun sleepovers? Roasting marshmallows around the campfire? Staying up late telling your friends scary stories? Or even desperately trying to keep a secret that you promised you would not share?

From childhood, stories captured our attention. And it hasn't changed. As adults, it's the stories that still make us stop, reflect, and share. People love stories and it's the stories that people connect with.

To be an effective storyteller on social media, you have to see each and every post, tweet, graphic and comment as a part of the larger story that is your business. Don't get caught up in the fallacy that social media is nothing but a distribution channel for what you have to offer.

Stories draw us in. They give us hope, they help us know we're not alone. Stories motivate us, move us, and challenge us.

When it comes to your business and ministry on social media, people will connect with you through your stories. People connect with people, not with brands.

Many businesses today have it mixed up when it comes to their social-media strategy and presence; many are turning people away. Social media is not a channel to broadcast products and services. Social media is about inviting people in through storytelling.

Social-media storytelling success comes when you can answer these questions clearly:

- **Who is your audience?** You have to have a clear understanding of who your audience is. What makes them laugh? What makes them cry? What pulls at their heartstrings? What questions do they have? What magazines do they read? What TV shows do they watch? What stores do they shop? What keeps them up at night? When you have a clear understanding of your audience, you can effectively share stories that they will want to engage with.

- **What story do you want to share through social media?** Do you know what your main message is? Do you know what your core story is? Every tweet, post, picture and comment tells the world who you are. What do you want readers to take from your story? Each one you share ought to have a takeaway for your audience, even if it's simply for a moment of lightness in their day.

- **What is the personality of your business?** How do you want to come across? Are you formal? Witty? Humorous? Laid back? Relaxed? Let your business or ministry personality shine. It will help readers know who you are, what you're about, and that you are trustworthy and real.

- **Where do want to share your story?** Where is your audience most active? Facebook? Twitter? Instagram? Pinterest? YouTube? LinkedIn? Snapchat? Which platform(s) are you most comfortable using? Make the most of the ones that you find yourself gravitating toward, as well as the ones your audience uses most. Your naturalness with it will serve as an asset. There may be a learning curve to using the ones your audience is on, if they aren't ones you're used to as much, but you can do it!

Storytelling is about sharing your human side and allowing people to understand and relate with you. It's sharing what you're doing, what you're learning, what you're thinking about. This is the art of storytelling.

Three experiences that I shared on one Facebook post show what I mean by the power of storytelling. Each of those stories centered on conflicts I'd had in business and ministry that not only challenged my heart's desire to lead, but ultimately held me back. Even to this day, each of them continues to try to hold me back from being all that God has created me to be. All showed a very real, vulnerable side of myself that I've learned can create connections with others and offer much-needed encouragement.

The caption on the included photo read "Ask God to reveal the truth of who He is and who He has created YOU to be so that regardless of what others say or think, deep down inside, you know who you are and who you belong to." People could relate to that. We long for belonging and the freedom to be ourselves. But we've all faced hurts that make us question whether we have what it takes, and whether others will view us as competent. And we value when others are real and open about their similar struggles.

In those three instances the lies of the enemy filled my mind. Lies about who I was and what I was called to do. I had to go back to God's truth to know what was real. Being real with Him and with other people ultimately strengthens us.

If you've found yourself in a similar situation, let me encourage you to ask God to reveal the truth of who He is and who He has created YOU to be. Let God work in you as He sets right the lies that you have been fed, with the truth of His word. And don't be discouraged at the time this will take; it will take time. But the end result is that regardless of what others say or think, deep down inside, you know where your true identity is. #BeReal #BeWorthFollowing

Share the real you with others and create a connection.

Utilize your story.

Do you realize the power of a ready-made story that's all yours to share? According to Phil Cooke, author of the book *Unique: Telling Your Story in the Age of Brands and Social Media*, "Creation stories tell the 'who' and the 'why' and give the consumer a basis for trust in the product."[4]

Each of us has a unique story to tell. I've shared pieces of mine already, but there's more to it that provides context to how I got to this point in my career and what motivates me to keep encouraging other women to build their platforms through social media.

Before it all began, I was sitting in Starbucks with my ministry team one day years ago. Before I knew it, words came out of the leader's mouth that struck me hard. I couldn't believe what I was hearing. It was in that instance that I knew, I was done. My time with the organization was over. I could no longer work in ministry with someone whose focus was on something that, deep down inside, I was so against.

The following year, at a completely different job, I was crying buckets of tears as my supervisor shared information that left me heartbroken. No, I wasn't laid off or fired; I was just deeply saddened with the way things were going. I was working all the time, giving my all, and again I was being told things that went against my values and beliefs. I was left thinking, is this really what business is all about?

Fast forward a few years and I was now the new face in the building. I quickly became known as the "hard" teacher. I actually made my students work. I made them read, write papers, complete their assignments. Before I knew it, I had parents complaining about me, stating that I had worked their children too hard, that I was being unfair, I ruined their child's opportunity for a scholarship, I didn't like the students. I was left wondering, "What are we teaching children if they don't learn now that they have to work at things? What are we teaching them if we always give them the easy way out? How will they ever survive in the real world?"

A year later, I disagreed with someone I respected and from whom I had learned. Because I disagreed with this person, I was immediately labeled a *religious Pharisee*. I was cast out of the group and this person refused to speak with me again.

And then, it happened again at a new job. Harsh words were spoken. I was surprised, hurt and angry. I gave them my all. I gave them my best. How could they do this to me, how could they talk to me this way, how could they treat me like this?

You may be asking right now, "Jen, what does this have to do with social media? What are you trying to say?" I promise it will all come together, so hang with me.

Social-media storytelling is about inspiring people to engage and share because they can relate to you. It's building a community, a relationship. It's a way of understanding one another. Anytime I share the story of how I have come to the place where I am right now, people are encouraged. People reach out, comment and engage. People start trusting me. The same can happen to you. The key is knowing your story and then sharing it online. Your story is powerful in God's hands.

Think about what these leaders are known for and the power of their stories: Billy Graham is the evangelist; Mother Teresa is about charity; Bethany Hamilton is about overcoming tragedy; Jenni Catron is the leadership woman. Their willingness to be open about their lives and God's life in them has been a powerful launching point for each one. They're all known for their various stories.

Like them, you have a story that needs to be shared. Do you believe it is powerful in God's hands? Here is what I want you to do. Before you move on to the next section, I want you to write down your story. How did you get to where you are right now? What led you here?

This story will help guide you and your business or ministry on a daily basis. This is the story that you will share with people all over social media. This is your story that will encourage the hearts of those who become a part of your community.

I promise, once you start sharing this story on social media, people will engage because stories move people.

Once you start sharing your story on social media, people will engage because stories move people.

Give people a reason to trust you.

Let's build on our realness through stories and talk about how being real can begin to build trust in our followers. How does that happen?

It's not uncommon for me to receive questions like this: *"I just started getting active on Facebook a week ago and I haven't made one sale yet. I'm confused and I'm not sure why no one is buying from me."*

Every time I get an email like this, it brings me back to a place when I first set out as an online entrepreneur.

I was working full-time as a middle-school teacher and was pursuing my life coaching business on the side. As the details of my very first website were coming together, I couldn't contain my excitement. I just knew as soon as my website went live, the calls and emails would begin pouring in for my services.

But as the weeks passed, I couldn't understand why I wasn't getting the business that I thought I would get. As a complete novice, I had no clue about keywords, SEO, branding, etc. I honestly thought people would just magically find me and immediately want to do business with me because, you know, I'm "likeable."

I soon learned it didn't work that way. And truthfully, it's the same thing with social media; people will not be social with you or do business with you until they have had the opportunity to get to know you and trust you. And friends, trust takes time.

- Trust Matters.
- Trust is what will build a community on social media.
- Trust is what will bring you a loyal fan base.
- Trust is what will bring you loyal customers.
- Trust is what will bring you revenue.
- Trust Matters.

As I mentioned, we'll talk more in depth about keeping trust in a later chapter, but I wanted to introduce it here because it's part of being real.

Social media takes time. It takes time to build your platforms. It takes time to truly understand your voice. It takes time to truly understand what differentiates you from everyone else who is doing what you are doing. It takes time to bring people into your community. It takes time to nurture it. It takes time to engage that community. It takes time for that community to feel comfortable engaging back with you. Building a thriving social-media community that eventually wants to do business with you, takes time.

I can't remember where I first heard it, but for years I've loved this quote from best-selling author and entrepreneur Seth Godin:

> *"Build it and they will come only works in the movies. Social media is a build it, nurture it, engage them and they may come and stay."*

All those things happen when we offer the real us online.

Tips from the front line
So what's with the #hashtag? Hashtags are one of the best "ideas" (in my honest opinion) that ever came to be! Hashtags are basically

a word or phrase that has a pound sign in front of it, much like #BeWorthFollowing.

- Hashtags allow your content and ideas to be found, but they also allow you to join other conversations around a specific hashtag. They can help create a brand awareness of YOU and they give you the opportunity to listen "socially" to what others are saying in your industry.
- One of the best things you can do is create your own branded hashtag around your story, your main message. Why? Because just like I've become known for the #BeWorthFollowing message, having your own hashtag can do the same for you.

Here are some tips to creating a successful, personal hashtag:

- Make it short
- Make it easy to spell
- Make it easy to remember
- Don't include any extra characters

Not only should you have your own hashtag, but also make sure that you know what the "popular" hashtags are in your industry that are being used on a regular basis. This will allow you to know what's happening in your niche and it will allow you to learn more about your niche, in addition to connecting with others.

Questions to consider

1. How did you get to where you are right now?
2. What's your story that you will share on social media?
3. How can you build trust online this week? Plan three action steps to implement in this area this week.

Tweetable moments

"People will not be social with you until they have had the opportunity to get to know you & trust you." ~@DrJenBennett, #BeWorthFollowing

Want to connect with your audience on a deeper level? Be Real. Be Authentic." ~@DrJenBennett, #BeWorthFollowing

"People want to get to know the REAL you!" ~@DrJenBennett, #BeWorthFollowing

"People will connect with you and your business through your stories." ~@DrJenBennett, #BeWorthFollowing

"People connect with people, not with brands." ~@DrJenBennett, #BeWorthFollowing

"Social Media is not about broadcasting; it's about inviting people in through storytelling." ~@DrJenBennett, #BeWorthFollowing

"Social-media storytelling is about inspiring people to engage & share because they can relate to you." ~@DrJenBennett, #BeWorthFollowing

"Every tweet, post, picture and comment tells the world who you are." ~@DrJenBennett, #BeWorthFollowing

"Every post, tweet, graphic and comment is a smaller part of the larger story that is your business." ~@DrJenBennett, #BeWorthFollowing

"Building a thriving social-media community that eventually wants to do business with you takes time." ~@DrJenBennett, #BeWorthFollowing

Chapter 7: #BeMissional
Remember the Kingdom Call

● ● ● ● ● ● ●

The Spirit of the Sovereign Lord is on me, because the *Lord* has anointed me to proclaim good news.

Isaiah 61:1, NIV

If there's one thing we can learn from browsing social media, it's that people all over the world are hurting. Take these headlines, for example:

- *Child Falls into Gorilla Cage*
- *Deadly Alligator Attack at Disney*
- *Deadliest Mass Shooting in American History*

Even now, writing these headlines causes my heart to sink. So much hurt, so much pain, so many questions and so many opinions.

So much vitriol. After each incident, our social-media newsfeeds were filled with story after story and comment after comment. As I scrolled through my feeds, what I saw were posts and comments filled with hate, pride, shame, blame and pointing of fingers. Comments and questions like:

- *Where were the parents? That would NEVER happen on my timetable!*
- *The parents should be charged!*
- *Lack of supervision!*
- *That would NEVER happen to me!*
- *This is what happens when you don't watch your kids!*

Added to all that, our country's recent and ongoing political turmoil has made a churning kettle out of social media, threatening to boil over from the constant commentary. Never-ending posts and comments filled with hate, pride, shame, blame and pointing of fingers are downright depressing.

These posts and comments snowball, and we're then bombarded with divisive (as opposed to constructive) arguments about gun laws, the presidency, the Supreme Court, the Constitution, refugees, the environment, the economy, life vs. choice, black lives versus white lives, marriage, minorities, the welfare system, the military, geo-engineering, animal lives, etc. It goes on and on. And if I'm honest with you, this is the part of social media that I really despise because that kind of division and destructiveness goes against everything that Jesus stands for, and it goes against everything that #BeWorthFollowing stands for.

We've become a society that thinks it's okay to point the finger behind the keyboard because it's easy to point, shame and blame behind a faceless screen; there's no accountability. But what isn't easy is getting up and doing something to help someone, to #BeDifferent and to go against the norms of culture. It's easy to write words, not so easy to take action.

Finger pointing behind a screen accomplishes NOTHING.

How many times have you heard (on Facebook no less) that Facebook is no longer fun? I know people who avoid it altogether now and have unfollowed many friends who can't keep a lid on their opinions. Twitter can be just as hostile an environment.

Granted, we all have a voice, and passivity can be as destructive as verbal assaults. So we feel guilty about not speaking up for God's truth and the only true hope that we know is found in him. But it's important to understand that there's a time and place and effective way to make our voices heard, right? We don't want to add to the noise and the chaos. We must pick our "battles" on social media, keeping in mind always that we are ambassadors for the Kingdom. How we behave online speaks for or against the holiness and love of our Father. With each post and comment we are building up or tearing down.

As believers we've got to ask ourselves what we can do to keep offering the all-powerful, eternal hope of Jesus that is the real answer this world needs. We need reminders of that hope ourselves if we're to survive (even thrive during) the time we spend on social-media platforms.

As Christians, we have been called to #BeDifferent. We have the Holy Spirit's healing to offer our hurting world. Many don't even know he is who they need first, more than any other solution. We should #BeWorthFollowing by offering healing words and Christ's truth and love (they do work simultaneously!). There should be something different about the way we react and respond online to tragedies, events, challenges and obstacles. Ultimately our goal for being online should be to #BeMissional, to share the hope and freedom that can be found in Jesus Christ alone. And in today's day and age, we have a great opportunity to do just that.

According to a survey that was conducted in May and June 2014 by the Pew Research Center, *"In an average week, one-in-five Americans share their religious faith online. And nearly half of U.S. adults see someone else share their religious faith online in a typical week. Fully 20% of Americans said they had shared their religious faith on social networking websites or apps (such as Facebook and Twitter) in the past week, and 46% said they had seen someone else share 'something about their religious faith' online."*

When I first saw these numbers, my immediate thought was that this needs to change. Yes, it's great that one in five Americans share their faith online, but if I'm honest with you, I think this needs to be higher and I think it can be higher. As more and more believers realize the impact they can have online as a #DigitalMissionary, the more of an impact we can make for the Kingdom of God.

Never has there been a time in our history when we have the opportunity to connect with people all over the world, instantly. And as online influencers we have a great opportunity to bring to life the words of the Great Commission that Jesus speaks to us in Matthew 28:19–20 (MSG):

> *Jesus, undeterred, went right ahead and gave his charge: "God authorized and commanded me to commission you: Go out and train everyone you meet, far and near, in this way of life, marking them by baptism in the threefold name: Father, Son, and Holy Spirit. Then instruct them in the practice of all I have commanded you. I'll be with you as you do this, day after day after day, right up to the end of the age."*

Before we can #BeMissional on social media, we have to realize that we have been commissioned by Jesus to go out and train everyone we meet, whether they are far or near. And this includes using our social-media influence and presence for good. Our profiles can't be all about us; they have to be bigger than who we are. As Christian women in business and ministry, our ultimate goal should be to lead others to a lasting relationship with Christ. Our voice should not be the loudest on #SocialMedia, but rather the voice of Jesus. And we can do that by sharing the ways and heart of Christ on social media. When we do, we are living out the Great Commission that we have been given.

7 Ways to Be Missional on Social Media

1. **Offer hope and encouragement:** Refuse to allow yourself to get caught up in the nonsense of arguments online. Social media should not be about having our voice be the loudest, but rather having the voice of Jesus shine through us. And one of the best ways to do this is by offering hope and encouragement on our profiles on a daily basis.

2. **Offer to pray for someone:** I've said this before, but people are hurting on social media. They are walking paths that they never imagined, and sometimes a prayer can make all the difference. Don't be afraid to reach out and let someone know that you are praying for him or her. And don't be afraid to write out your prayer for them. I've had women do this for me and I can't even begin to explain the difference it made in my life that day.

3. **Become known for whom you're for, rather than what you're against:** There are FAR too many posts on social media that scream everything we're against. Is it no wonder some people have a sour taste in their mouth when it comes to the followers of Christ? Instead, let's become known for whom we are for: Jesus Christ. Instead of spewing what we're against, let's share why we are a Christ follower and how He changed our lives for the better.

4. **Share how God is speaking to you:** Don't be afraid to share what God is showing you and speaking to you. Many

times what He shows you is something that others need to be shown too. Be real. Be authentic. Be transparent.

5. **Be Intentional:** Being missional on social media doesn't just happen, it requires being intentional. It means thinking before you post and comment. It means seeing your platforms in a new light; a light that shines on Jesus and not always you. It means thinking about others before thinking about you. It means seeing your platforms as an opportunity to serve others on a daily basis.

6. **Turn your words into action:** On social media, it can be so easy to respond to cries for help with "I'm praying for you" or "thinking about you." But what if that cry for help needed more than just a statement saying that you are praying for them? What if that cry for help comes from someone local who needs action behind your words? Or what if that cry for help comes from someone who needs a word of encouragement via a letter or card or maybe even a gift certificate to help them get back on their feet? Don't be afraid to turn your words into action.

7. **Remember it is not our job to change people:** Our role is to pray and speak (or write) as prompted by the Holy Spirit, not on our own initiative or "wisdom." The work of change in anyone's heart and mind is God's role. The weight of changing minds is not ours to carry, which is a great thing, thank the Lord! We live and speak and click our keyboards for Him, being available for Him to use, while He does the behind-the-scenes heart work in other people's lives.

There are SO many barriers in our world that are keeping people from coming to know and experience Christ. Maybe they had a bad experience with the church, maybe they're fearful of what people will think, maybe they question whether or not the church will accept them, or maybe they are housebound due to illness. Whatever the issue is, you have the opportunity to impact them positively as an online influencer, to breathe life and hope into the people who are watching everything you write and everything you share. You could be instrumental in God breaking down a wall that someone has been holding on to far too long. You just might be the person God wants to use to do just that!

Our #SocialMedia goal is to share the hope & freedom that can be found in Christ alone, to #BeMissional.

Friend, don't take your online leadership lightly. People are watching and people are wondering if you are worth following. We have been given much and we have a big responsibility when it comes to our online influence. Remember, you've been called to reach the nations for Christ; social media gives you the opportunity to do just that.

(More to come about fending off the enemy's onslaught when we threaten his dirty work with the Gospel!)

Tips from the front line

As I mentioned before, one of the keys to social-media success involves you making the first move, connecting with people first. Here are a few tips on how to do just that:

- Once you know the hashtags in your industry, search them out on Facebook, Twitter and Instagram. Find people who are using them too and connect with them.
- What conferences take place in your niche? Many of those conferences have specific hashtags. Find people who are using those hashtags and connect with them.

- Many of the social-media platforms allow you to search your email contacts on their platforms to see if those people are on the platform too. Take advantage of this.
- Many of the platforms will also recommend people you should connect with. Take a look at those recommendations and see if those people would be a good fit.
- Use Facebook and Twitter advertising to find people in your target audience. When you really know your target audience (age, demographics, what they like, who they follow, what they read, etc.) you can really target those people through advertising. This is a great way to connect with people who most likely will be interested in connecting with you.
- Create a group on Facebook that is public and allows people to join. Make this a group where you provide even more value and where people can have the opportunity to get to know you better.
- Create a list in Twitter of the people you want to get to know. Follow the people you put on that list and engage with them on a regular basis.
- Allow people to follow you on your personal profile on Facebook. What this means is that they can follow you without being "friends" with you. They will only see the public posts that you share.
- Be sure to include a link to your Facebook business page on your personal profile in the Intro/About section. Make it easy for people to learn more about your business/ministry.

Questions to consider

1. When have you forced yourself to remain quiet when a social-media post has angered or depressed you? When have you made your voice heard?
2. How can you use social media to lead others to Christ?

3. How can you offer love and hope to the hurting cries of others?
4. Who do you need to reach out to today, online?
5. Give yourself a social-media audit: Are the majority of your posts about you or about the God you serve? What may need to change?

Tweetable moments

"It's easy to write words, not so easy to take action." ~@DrJenBennett, #BeWorthFollowing

"Finger pointing behind a screen accomplishes NOTHING." ~@DrJenBennett, #BeWorthFollowing

"The way we react & respond to online to tragedies should #BeDifferent." ~@DrJenBennett, #BeWorthFollowing

"Our #SocialMedia goal is to share the hope & freedom that can be found in Christ alone; to #BeMissional." ~@DrJenBennett, #BeWorthFollowing

"You can make an impact online for the Kingdom of God as a #DigitalMissionary." ~@DrJenBennett, #BeWorthFollowing

"We have been commissioned by Jesus to go out and train everyone we meet, to #BeMissional online." ~@DrJenBennett, #BeWorthFollowing

"Our voice should not be the loudest on #SocialMedia, but rather the voice of Jesus." ~@DrJenBennett, #BeWorthFollowing

"Let's become known for whom we are for on social media, Jesus Christ." ~@DrJenBennett, #BeWorthFollowing

"Being missional on social media doesn't just happen, it requires being intentional." ~@DrJenBennett, #BeWorthFollowing

"You could be instrumental in God breaking down a wall on #SocialMedia that someone has had for too long." ~@DrJenBennett, #BeWorthFollowing

"You've been called to reach the nations for Christ; #SocialMedia gives you the opportunity to do that." ~@DrJenBennett, #BeWorthFollowing

Chapter 8: #BeDiscerning
For Heaven's Sake, Filter!

Now teach me good judgment as well as knowledge. For your laws are my guide.

Psalm 119:66, TLB

Jumping off the concept of #BeMissional, it bears repeating how much we need to use discernment about when and how and what to post as online missionaries. Because our every word and action reflects the name of Jesus, we need to continually ask Him to give us the words He wants us to share. And—this is critical—we need to practice the "spiritual pause" when we sense His check on our spirit telling us that what we are about to share is not from His own Spirit. No matter how tempting it is, no matter how wrong we think someone else's post is, no matter how right the side we are fighting for.

Sometimes the fight or response is not ours to make. At least outwardly. When the Spirit checks yours as your fingers hover over the keyboard with an "oh-so-right comeback," take the issue inward to God in prayer instead of letting your fingers fly across the keys. Don't let your humanness get the better of you online; put every potential post and comment through God's filter first.

If there is a conflict, fight the fight vertically with Him, not horizontally, in human ways on earth. When He tells us to let Him handle the battle, we need to back off and leave it with Him. He is constantly working in ways we can't see in order to bring about His plans and draw others to Him. There are times we get in the way and complicate things when we try to do his job for Him.

Even if there's no conflict involved, some comments simply aren't wise. As human beings, we are prone to speak too much, to share too many opinions, and to be too sure of our own "righteous" views about a situation. It's in our default wiring to spout off too much, to our own downfall. That's why we needed the Savior in the first place, not just for eternal security to save us from ourselves, but for daily living for Him. When left to our own devices, we will mess up eventually. Every one of us. Guaranteed. So get comfortable with His filter in your spirit and online.

There's a lot at stake, so we must #BeDiscerning.

Your posts are either opening doors for you or closing them shut. We have to be very discerning when it comes to our online influence. We have to stop and think before we post and before we respond to a comment. Part of being someone who is worth following is someone who knows what it means to #BeDiscerning.

Influential people are watching your platforms, and it isn't just about the clients who purchase your products and service. What about the director who wants to hire you to speak at their event? The CEO who wants you to come in and share your expertise with their organization? The business owner who wants you to guest post on their blog or in their magazine? The literary agent who's looking to partner with you for your first or tenth book?

Here are some of the most common social-media "deadly sins" that are causing far too many business women to miss out on opportunities that could have been theirs, had they been more discerning with their posts and comments:

Social-media "deadly sins"

1. **Being too emotional:** Yes, we all have those people in our lives who rub us the wrong way, but please know that social media is not the place to air all of your dirty laundry. You may be trying to prove a point via your post; but truthfully, all it's doing is making you look bad. And we all have days (and even seasons) when our emotions seem to take over our logic, but too much sharing can make people question who they're dealing with. No doubt you have seen posts that made you want to holler, "For the love—*filter!*" Yeah, you don't want to be that person. Even when your own words don't sound bad to you, just like texts and emails leave room for misunderstandings in tone, so do too many emotional posts.

2. **Taking part in online conflicts:** Here are some questions to ask yourself: Is this really going to matter in the long run? Is this your fight to fight? Is it that important to get your point across or to have the last word? Does the online world really need to see and read this? Is this conflict worth me losing a client or opportunity over? Social media is not the place for conflicts. All it does is make you look bad. Avoid them at all costs.

3. **Trying to separate your personal and professional life:** We would like to believe that we can separate our personal and professional lives online, but it's not possible. Everything you do and say reflects who you are as an individual and who you are as a professional. What you do on a daily basis gives insight into you as a business owner. What you say gives insight into how you will communicate with clients. Don't fall for the lie that these two areas can be separated; they just can't.

4. **Complaining about your clients:** Unfortunately, this is becoming the norm; I see it every day. And what most professionals don't realize is that it's closing doors for them on a regular basis. The director for that dream speaking engagement may have been interested in you and learning more about you, but as soon as you posted that negative, whiny complaint about your client, that door immediately shut. And then you're left wondering why doors keep closing for you.

5. **Being pushy:** Want to lose the interest of people quickly? Post on their Facebook wall about your upcoming event, product, service, webinar, etc. Nothing aggravates people more than business owners who become pushy when it comes to their business. Also, don't send direct messages to people you have never engaged with or have hardly engaged with, telling them about your business. This will get you ignored and put a sour taste about you and your business in their mind.

6. **Insulting others:** Your posts should not destroy people, but instead, encourage and lift them up. One of the most important skills to have on social media is the ability to "talk" to others who disagree with you. Please don't act like a child by name calling, insulting, and destroying people. Remember, you don't have to attend every discussion that takes place online. You be different. You be the one who takes the higher road.

7. **Being manipulative:** Before posting, always ask yourself, "Am I posting this because I hope 'that someone' will see my post?" Are you secretly trying to get back at someone via your social-media posts? Are you secretly trying to "say something" to that "someone" through your posts? If so, don't post. Your motives are not right, and you are not bringing honor to God.

Ultimately, He knows your heart and why you are posting the things that you are posting.

There are so many opportunities available to you, and people are watching to see if you are a good fit for what they are looking for. We know what some of the deadly online sins are—what not to do. How about some positive things to do?

Tips for using discernment:

1. **Limit Your Time:** We tell ourselves we'll hop onto Facebook for just a few minutes, and when we look up, we realize we just wasted two hours of our life. Why not use a timer? If you want to be on social media for fifteen minutes, set your timer and once it rings, log off and go about your day. No looking back!

2. **Be intentional in choosing online connections:** You don't have to be friends with everyone on social media. If you find that someone with whom you've connected has nothing but depressing, argumentative, whiny posts—go ahead, disconnect from them. Surround yourself with positive people who offer something valuable in their social-media feeds.

3. **Be a shining light online:** It starts with YOU. You can make the decision to be different—to use social media in a positive way. You can encourage, inspire, and give hope on a daily basis. You can choose not to get involved in arguments online or complain about things in your life. You can choose to be different.

4. **Give it to God:** I know how hard it is to see the stories online of people who have passed away, people fighting cancer, disease, sickness, and stories of children being hurt or

missing. It can and does get to you. When you see these stories, stop and take a minute to pray for that person or that family. Immediately give it over to God and ask Him to make a way. Don't try to carry the burden on your own. You can also ask Him to make it crystal clear to you if He wants you to help in a tangible way.

Social media can be a great tool if we want to impact the lives of others in a positive way. We just have to decide how we will use it, and realize our uniqueness and the unique story that God wants to share through us.

As I write this, I'm reminded of a message I received one day from someone who decided to move forward and take part in my Social Media Managers Training Course that I was offering. Her email said,

"I just want you to know that over the past weekend, I realized how much you have taught me over the last few years. That's all been by watching you online, and I am truly inspired and 'want to be you when I grow up!'"

This client, who I now consider a friend, was watching me from afar for years before she ever decided to do "business" with me. She was watching what I wrote, what I shared and how I responded to comments. And after a few years of doing this, she decided to move forward with what I offered. And this isn't the only example. I can't tell you how many times people have sent me a message stating that they have been "watching for years."

Remember, #BeDiscerning. People are watching you too. They are checking to see if you are worth following. And if you win their trust, then not only will they become a client, but they might become a friend too.

Tips from the front line

One of the keys to social-media success is actively using some third-party apps that make your life just a bit easier. Here are some of my favorites:

- Hootsuite for Twitter scheduling and engagement
- Meet Edgar for creating queues that allow content to be shared on a regular basis on my Twitter account
- Canva for graphic creation for my social-media platforms
- Grum or Schedugram for Instagram scheduling
- Unsplash for free graphics that you can download and use
- Lightstock for graphics that you can use in ministry
- Stocksy for graphics that are "cheesy free"

Questions to consider

1. Which of the "deadly sins" above do you struggle with the most?
2. What changes can you promise yourself today to make when it comes to that "deadly sin"?
3. What doors of opportunity are you wanting God to open for you?
4. Are your social-media platforms giving you the opportunity to open those doors? Why or why not?

Tweetable moments

"Influential people are watching your platforms. Your posts will open doors for you or close them shut." ~@DrJenBennett, #BeWorthFollowing

"Part of being someone who is worth following, is someone who is discerning." ~@DrJenBennett, #BeWorthFollowing

"Social media is not the place for conflicts. All it does is make you look bad. Avoid them at all costs." ~@DrJenBennett, #BeWorthFollowing

"Everything you do and say reflects who you are as an individual and who you are as a professional." ~@DrJenBennett, #BeWorthFollowing

"Your Social-media posts should not destroy people, but instead, encourage and lift them up." ~@DrJenBennett, #BeWorthFollowing

"You don't have to attend every online discussion. #BeDifferent and take the higher road." ~@DrJenBennett, #BeWorthFollowing

"You don't have to be friends with everyone on social media!" ~@DrJenBennett, #BeWorthFollowing

Part III: Growing Pains

Social-media growth will involve challenges, with numbers, with our own limitations, with spiritual forces as we aim to build Jesus' Kingdom. Let's develop our strategies so we're ready for the ups and downs.

Chapter 9: #BeEnduring
Building Consistent Trust That Lasts

We continually ask God to fill you with the knowledge of his will through all the wisdom and understanding that the Spirit gives, so that you may live a life worthy of the Lord and please him in every way: bearing fruit in every good work, growing in the knowledge of God, being strengthened with all power according to his glorious might so that you may have great endurance.

Colossians 1:9–11, NIV

Being social on social media requires that you not only build a foundation that will last, but that you also become someone who is trustworthy and someone who is expert in your field. When you know who you are, where you're going, and what you have to offer, you will become a trusted source others will want to engage with and do business with. You will #BeEnduring.

But the path most likely won't be smooth. It's been said over and over again that most things worth fighting for will not come easily. Online success is no different.

We'll get to success later, but for now let's focus on what it means to develop an online presence that goes the distance. What does that require? Part of success involves being sustainable, not merely offering a fleeting benefit. That all sounds great, right?

But sometimes we can feel stalled, even though it seems we're doing everything right. Sometimes if feels as if we've been dropped off in the middle of nowhere, and we don't know what to do next, and we question whether we heard God correctly.

The power of the wilderness

I have a confession to make. I really like survivor-type reality TV shows. Let me share a few characteristics of these programs:

- In many instances, men and women are dropped off in the middle of nowhere and are left to survive on their own for multiple days at a time.
- They have NOTHING. No food, no water, no shelter and in some cases, no clothes. Yikes!
- The goal? To see if you can survive with nothing.
- They are surrounded by wildlife, including BIG cats. There are no guarantees of safety.
- People who are VERY different surround them on a daily basis. They have to learn to get along together.

I'll admit, these shows really intrigue me. I'm amazed at how people can survive when they have nothing. As I watch these shows, I often wonder if I would survive even one day. Honestly, I would probably roll up in a ball and cry. I just don't want to be left alone in the wilderness, hungry, scared and fighting for my life.

But there definitely have been times when I was trying to grow my influence on social media, when I knew I was doing everything right: following, engaging, posting. But I felt like doors for speaking and consulting were not opening up. I'd wonder how all those other people who weren't doing all the things I was doing; how in the world were they getting all those speaking engagements and new clients, but I wasn't? I felt like I was in a sort of wilderness.

I was sad, upset, questioning everything. I recall talking with my husband, Luke, and asking why such-and-such professor was speaking about social media at a conference, when he had only fifty Twitter followers! Why weren't opportunities like that opening up for me more?

Can you relate?

Well, I've kept Luke's encouragement with me and want to offer it to you as well. He said, "Jen, don't worry about it. Just keep doing your thing. Just keep moving forward."

It's true that our hard work feels the hardest when we can check all the to-do boxes and know we're doing all we can … without much to show for it. Now I realize God was preparing me through that season. I look back and see it as a wilderness time of preparation, and I can be thankful.

God shows a pattern in his Word of preparing His followers before launching them. Abraham had to wait years for the fulfillment of God's promise of a son. Noah spent years building an ark. John the Baptist spent years in a literal wilderness. Paul's traveling missionary ministry didn't begin until after a time of training with the Lord. And even Jesus spent three decades preparing for a three-year ministry.

As I've watched survivor programs, I can't help but think of Jesus and His wilderness experience right before He entered into His public ministry. In Matthew 4:13–17, we read about Jesus being baptized by John. And as He came up from the water, the heavens opened and He saw the spirit of God descending like a dove. And then He heard the voice of God say, "This is My beloved Son, in whom I am well pleased."

What a moment that must have been, to know that God your Father is well pleased with you.

But, if you keep reading, Matthew 14:1 says, "Then Jesus was led up by the Spirit into the wilderness to be tempted by the devil." Okay, what just happened? Everything was looking awesome, and now Jesus is headed into the wilderness to be tempted by the devil? That sounds more like a punishment than a reward from a God who says He is well pleased. And not only was Jesus in the wilderness, but He was fasting; He was hungry. And of course, the devil took advantage of this; he tempted Jesus for forty days. There were three specific temptations that Jesus encountered in the wilderness:

- The temptation to meet a real need (like hunger) in a wrong way
- The temptation to "use" God for his own benefit
- The temptation to take a shortcut towards power and fame

Take a moment to think this through. Is it any surprise that Satan would tempt Jesus while He's hungry and right before He enters into His public ministry, in these three specific ways? I truly believe that Satan was doing whatever he could to keep Jesus from moving forward into the assignment, the calling, and the ministry that He was called to. Satan wanted to destroy Jesus and the influence that he knew He would have. And guess what? I know that Satan wants to do the same thing to those of us who have been called.

I honestly believe that when God calls us, we will experience a time in the "wilderness." A time when we're tired, weak and really questioning whether or not God has called us. It's a time when we start wondering if we really heard God. We've tried to move forward but obstacles keep popping up. People keep trying to convince us to go in another direction. The funds are running low. And really, there are more questions than there are answers. And the tiredness has set in. You're ready to throw in the towel (just like many do on the survivor-type shows).

But if you take a moment to think this through, isn't it interesting that Jesus went through this wilderness experience right before He launched His public ministry? And yet, He didn't give in to the temptations of the enemy. Instead, He proclaimed the Word of God back to the enemy. And after the third temptation and hearing the Word of God for the third time, Scripture says, "Then the devil left Him and behold, angels came and ministered to Him" (Matthew 4:11).

What does this have to do with us? Actually, quite a bit:

- **The wilderness helps prepare you for your God assignment:** As much as I don't like wilderness experiences, I know they are necessary. It is through these experiences that we not only draw closer to God, but we become fully aware of our need for Christ and what it is that we are really made of.
- **The enemy will come at you when you are at your weakest:** It isn't surprising that the enemy took advantage of Jesus' hunger. And guess what? He does the same with us. When he sees us at our weakest, when we start questioning and doubting everything, you can bet that he's going to come in and start messing with our minds.
- **The Word of God is vital to overcoming the lies of the enemy:** Jesus combated the enemy by proclaiming the Word of God at every temptation that was thrown to Him. This is key for us. If we want to resist the lies that the enemy is feeding us, we must be prepared today. We must know the Word of God. This is the one thing that will keep us from falling prey to his schemes.
- **The wilderness will cause you to see and know what you really believe:** It's easy to say we believe in God, but when things get tough, do we really act out on what we believe? Do we really believe God and what He has shared with us? If He's called us, then we will not give in to the lies that the enemy tries to feed us to keep us from moving forward.

- **There is more at stake than you can see right now:** Andy Stanley says that every time you are tempted, there are three things at stake: your future, someone else's future and your faith. When temptation comes, you only see the here and now. But truthfully, there are so many other things that are riding on your decision to give in or power through:

  1. **Your calling**: If you give in to the lies that claim God didn't really call you, your future is at stake. You'll end up living a life that God never intended for you to live. Instead of experiencing all that God had for you, you'll live a life that is less than fulfilling.

  2. **Someone else's future**: God gives each of us a calling not for our benefit, but for the benefit of others and, ultimately, to bring Him praise and glory. Take seriously all the ways He wants to reach other people through you. Don't give up your calling due to the lies of the enemy, and see how He will work in your own life as a result.

  3. **Your Faith**: The wilderness experience allows you to put action to your words, your belief, and your faith. Your faith will either grow during this time period or shrivel up.

My point? Don't negate the importance of the wilderness. It's vital to your usability for God's purposes. Stay connected to him, keep doing what He asks each day. The last thing you'd want it to strike out on your own without being ready, according to His timeline and wisdom. Continue being faithful even when you don't see the results you'd hoped for. There's more going on from God's point of view than you can see right now.

When the feedback isn't positive

By now we know we may face seasons when we don't get much feedback. But what happens when you receive negative feedback or find yourself in a season when everything and everyone seems to be working against you?

First, let's revisit the trust angle we already covered. We've touched on developing trust. Now let's think over how to keep trust, to be enduring even when hit with negative feedback and other hurdles. How do you keep trust on social media so your community continues wanting to be social with you and do business with you? Here are some thoughts:

Keeping their faith:

1. **Be consistent:** Honestly, there is nothing worse than heading over to a business' profile and realizing that their posting is sporadic. They haven't posted in the last two months, or they are posting once a week only. When I see inconsistency like this, I don't like the page, I don't follow, and ultimately I don't do business with them. Why? Because if they are inconsistent on their profiles, how can I trust them to be consistent with me as a customer?

2. **Be human:** Want to know a pet peeve of mine? When "influencers" consistently share how much money they have made, the lists they have been on, how many people are following them, etc. Yes, I get it: You are seen as an expert, influencer, guru, etc. But quite honestly, that doesn't make me trust you even more. What allows me to trust you is your humanness. Are you someone I can relate to? Are you someone I can talk to? Are you someone who will engage back with me? Do you share your failures along with your successes? Are you human? Or has your "influence" caused you to lose sight of all the other "regular" people out there who are trying to make it and trying to live a life of purpose? For me, being human is a BIG deal. Want people to feel the same way about you? Don't be afraid to be your true self. Don't be afraid to be human.

3. **Be transparent:** One of the best ways to be transparent is to not delete every single negative comment that you get (and believe me, you will get some). When people share a negative comment or review on your platforms, you have wonderful opportunities to share and show what you are really made of. I can promise you, by the time you decide to delete a comment, people have already seen it. When they realize that it's gone, they will be left wondering what really happened and questioning whether or not they should do business with you. Friends, negative comments give you the opportunity to #BeDifferent, to #BeEnduring and to #BeWorthFollowing.

4. **Grow your skills:** The bar is already set high on social media, and each of us has a responsibility to give our best and become as knowledgeable as we can be in our field. Each of us has the opportunity to become an expert, and we ought to pursue excellence. A halfway job isn't going to cut it. Aim as high as you can, and be a lifelong learner. And remember, you must be willing to do whatever it takes to get good at your craft so that you can stand out and be the best.

5. **Respond constructively to negative feedback:** You will get negative feedback. I could callously tell you to get used to it, but that wouldn't be gracious of me. Instead, I'll gently encourage you ... to get used it. And develop the grace and discernment to know how to respond in ways that turn the tables on someone's negativity. Surprise them with grace, which is sorely lacking in our world. Proverbs 15:1 (MSG) says, "A gentle response diffuses anger, but a sharp tongue kindles a temper-fire." Your other followers (who are noticing the negative responses) may not remember every negative comment, but they will remember your consistent, enduring tone of grace. Respond, don't react. Refuse to sink to someone else's

level, and instead raise the bar on a conversation that is heading downhill. Don't be dragged down; instead, lift up. Honor their concern. In fact, thinking of a negative comment as someone's genuine concern instead of as an attack will keep you on a thoughtful path instead of a reactionary one that tempts you to attack back. Having a tough skin, but not a harsh one—a thick skin that is strengthened by grace—will earn you the respect of others, not to mention you'll please the Lord.

You might be surprised to know that your helpful response to a negative comment may actually earn you more followers. I LOVE this from Jay Baer: *"While only 41 percent of people who complain on Facebook, Twitter, Yelp, TripAdvisor, and other review sites anticipate a response, when they do* receive a response, they're almost twice as likely to recommend the company afterward."[5]

One time someone messaged me to say they loved how I responded to people. Even though I was straightforward, I was always kind and gracious. You bet I took that person's words seriously and still make sure to filter my responses with grace.

Social media can be challenging since the nature of having a screen between us and others can create a boldness, or even an attitude, that we wouldn't normally use face-to-face. We need to take care every time on social media so we don't react impulsively and hurt someone else.

Social media can bring out the best in people—and the worst. No matter who you are, you're going to face times when friends or followers will inflame you with their well-aimed jabs or judgments.

This happens to everyone who puts themselves out there on social media. But you don't have to react to negative comments as though a crisis is taking place. Instead, you can choose to see the negativity as something you can build upon. Let's add more defense armor to our arsenal to #BeEnduring online.

More tips on responding to negativity on social media:

1. **Remember that not everyone will like you:** This is something we all have to come to terms with. There are those who love us and then those who would rather not know us. And that's okay. That's why it's important to have a clear understanding of who your target audience is.

2. **Maintain professionalism:** Never allow a negative comment to throw you off track to the point where you lose your professionalism. People are watching—and people are watching even more when there seems to be a disagreement taking place. Always choose the higher road, because if you don't, it will come back to bite you.

3. **Never label people who disagree with you:** I have seen this before, and when I do I can't help but cringe. You typically don't fully know the commenter, so to label them as something is not only unprofessional, but just plain rude. Again, people are watching, and if they see you labeling someone, you may have just lost an important contact.

4. **Resist the urge to respond to every comment:** While I'm a big fan of engaging with your audience on social media, I also believe that there are times when it is best to remain quiet (remember our #BeDiscerning tips). When you do, you give your followers the opportunity to speak up, and many times those fans will speak up on your behalf.

5. **Resist the urge to respond right away:** If you choose to respond, let me encourage you to give yourself time. There have been times in my own life when, if I would have waited a bit to

respond to something, my words and actions would have been quite different and for the better. I'll never forget one time I responded too quickly, and the woman thought I was calling her a liar. If I had paused before typing my response, there's a good chance I would have taken more care with my choice of words. Sometimes you simply need to sleep on something before you speak up. Take your time and don't rush into it.

6. **Don't call people out when they disagree with you:** I've seen this happen too many times. Take the higher road. In the end, you'll look better for it. And your character will grow in endurance because of it.

7. **Always be respectful and polite:** Sometimes the written word can be taken the wrong way. Give others the benefit of the doubt. And regardless of whether or not they meant what they wrote, always choose to respond with respect and polite words. It's hard to argue with someone who continually shows respect.

8. **Lighten up:** Sometimes I think we're too serious, and anytime someone criticizes or disagrees with us, we're either hurt or ready to pounce. I once read a comment on someone's Facebook fan page where they were telling the business owner to "chill out" because the business owner was over-reacting to something that really wasn't a big deal. Putting ourselves out there in public comes with criticism. We have to train ourselves to roll with it!

Choose to focus on the impact you're making, and know that not everyone is going to approve of everything you say. Remaining positive and refusing to engage in social-media battles will gain and keep the respect of followers, and keep your reputation spotless.

In addition to being gracious in the face of negativity, what else can we do to #BeEnduring? Sometimes the uphill climb to increase our enduring impact on social media has nothing to do with surviving negative feedback, which seems like defensive action.

Take charge! Proactive tips to #BeEnduring:

1. **Share stories:** Story telling is a must, as we discussed earlier. This is how people will connect with you. Don't be afraid to share where you have been, where you have come from and what your mistakes have taught you. This goes back to being human. When you share your stories, you are bringing a human element to your business and this is what draws people to you.

2. **Give value:** Want to be seen as someone who is trustworthy and someone who knows what they are talking about? Share GREAT content and provide GREAT value. Far too often I see businesses on social media sharing "stuff" that no one really cares about. If you want to be seen as the authority in your niche, you have to provide great content. People need to see that you really do know what you are talking about. The more you share, the more people will come to trust you. And don't just repost what other experts are saying. Come up with your own material, and be the expert the other experts what to repost!

3. **Connect with real people:** Don't wait for people to find you. Seek out people. You be the first to engage with them. And when I say engage, I mean really engaging with them. Don't try to sell them. Just engage. Get to know them. If you wait for people to engage with you first, you will be waiting a long time.

4. **Stay engaged:** As people engage with you, be sure to respond. Try not to leave people hanging. There is nothing worse than starting a conversation with someone online and then never returning to continue the conversation. Again, if you want people to engage with you, you have to be willing to take the time and engage with them. Remember that people crave connection, to belong. Let them know they are welcome in your tribe.

5. **Make it about others:** Want to know another one of my pet peeves? When you connect with someone on Twitter and they immediately try to get you to download their eBook, check out their video, buy their book or engage with them on another platform. Please don't do this. If you truly want people to engage with you, you not only have to seek them out first, but you have to make it about them. Don't make it about you and what you have to offer. Another one of our human default wiring characteristics is that we are inherently self-centered. We are givers, sure. But we also want to know what's in it for us. So get to know others. Ask them questions. Look at their business. Ask them what they do. Again, it's about them, not you.

6. **Make customer service a priority:** We've all seen it; more and more people are using social media for customer service. If something goes wrong or if they have a question, their first stop is social media. No matter how big or small your business is, customer service on your social-media platforms has to be a priority. If people come to your platforms and there are no responses to questions, people will not follow you, and they will not do business with you. Want people to see that you care? Respond to their inquiries on your platforms.

On our path to #BeEnduring, we've covered keeping trust, responding to negative feedback, and proactive steps we can take to show people our platforms are ones to keep following. But those skills aren't all we need to be long-lasting as an online leader in our field.

What about spiritual warfare?

We've got to come to terms that believers committed to Christ's Kingdom are instant targets of forces behind our human world. Spiritual warfare is real, and it's real in your business or ministry. You need to be armed with the biblical weapons of spiritual warfare and alert to the reality of them in your social-media life.

How the enemy tries to thwart your impact:

- By distracting you regarding your ultimate purpose—to promote God's platform
- By convincing you that success is all about numbers
- By distracting you about God's definition of true success
- By distracting you to believe God's definition of success isn't yours to have
- By lying to you about your usefulness
- By lying to you that your abilities are too limited
- By lying to you that your abilities are enough without leaning on God
- By distracting you to waste too much time on social media
- By working on your emotions when you read negative feedback
- By working on your emotions when you read angry or depressing posts
- By convincing you that everyone is against you
- By reminding you of past failures
- By confusing you about priorities: God, family, business/ministry
- By distracting you with comparing yourself to anyone else
- By distracting you from your daily business meeting with God
- By causing you to forget the power of prayer

The list goes on! As believers we're in a 24/7 battle with unseen forces in the heavenly realm, and we are not equipped to fight them in our own power. But God knows the work He wants to accomplish through each of us, and He wants to empower and guard us to do our part effectively. Securing ourselves to Him is the most important key to being enduring. He is able to guard us, and His plans through us will endure.

> *God is strong, and he wants you strong. So take everything the Master has set out for you, well-made weapons of the best materials. And put them to use so you will be able to stand up to everything the Devil throws your way. This is no afternoon athletic contest that we'll walk away from and forget about in a couple of hours. This is for keeps, a life-or-death fight to the finish against the Devil and all his angels. Be prepared. You're up against far more than you can handle on your own. Take all the help you can get, every weapon God has issued, so that when it's all over but the shouting you'll still be on your feet. Truth, righteousness, peace, faith, and salvation are more than words. Learn how to apply them. You'll need them throughout your life.*

God's Word is an indispensable weapon. In the same way, prayer is essential in this ongoing warfare. Pray hard and long. Pray for your brothers and sisters. Keep your eyes open. Keep each other's spirits up so that no one falls behind or drops out.

Ephesians 6:10–12, MSG

Tips from the front line
Can Facebook ads work for you? Let's see.
- If your budget allows, set up a budget of $10 a day.
- Create a variety of ads that will allow you to test and see which one is responding the best. Create ads with the same copy but different graphics and vice versa.

- Wait at least 24–48 hours before you stop any ads. Give them time to work.
- Create different ads for your different audiences. When you do, you'll see better results because you're creating copy and visuals that speak to that specific audience.
- Try not to use any copy in your ad graphic. Facebook tends to show ads that have no copy in the graphic, more often.
- Make sure that your graphic goes along with the copy in your ad. They must work together.
- Know what your goal is for the ad. What is your objective? Be super clear about this.
- Stay focused with the copy in your ad. The shorter the better. Keep it simple. Don't talk about you, but rather share value and benefits.

Questions to consider

1. Have you faced a wilderness preparation time in your life? In what areas did you experience growth through it?
2. Are you keeping your online community's trust? How?
3. Was there a time when you wish you had responded to a post or comment differently? What did you learn from that experience?
4. How have you experienced spiritual warfare in your business or ministry?
5. What proactive steps will you take this week to #BeEnduring on social media?

Tweetable moments

"You don't have to react to negative comments on social media as though a crisis is taking place." ~@DrJenBennett, #BeWorthFollowing

"Be willing to do whatever it takes to get good at your craft so that you can stand out & be the best." ~@DrJenBennett, #BeWorthFollowing

"Never allow a negative comment to throw you off track to the point where you lose your professionalism." ~@DrJenBennett, #BeWorthFollowing

"Inconsistency on social media gives the impression that you are inconsistent with your customers." ~@DrJenBennett, #BeWorthFollowing

"Negative comments on social media give you the opportunity to #BeDifferent, to #BeEnduring and to #BeWorthFollowing." ~@DrJenBennett

"No matter how big or small your business is, customer service on social media has to be a priority." ~@DrJenBennett, #BeWorthFollowing

"Don't be afraid to share where you have been and what your mistakes have taught you." ~@DrJenBennett, #BeWorthFollowing

"God knows the work he wants to accomplish through each of us, and he wants to empower and guard us to do our part effectively." ~@DrJenBennett, #BeWorthFollowing

Chapter 10: #BePractical #BeDetermined, #BeFocused, #BeOrganized, #BeResourceful

● ● ● ● ● ● ●

All the women whose hearts stirred them to use their skill spun the goats' hair. And the leaders brought onyx stones and stones to be set, for the ephod and for the breastpiece, and spices and oil for the light, and for the anointing oil, and for the fragrant incense. All the men and women, the people of Israel, whose heart moved them to bring anything for the work that the Lord *had commanded by Moses to be done brought it as a freewill offering to the* Lord.

Exodus 35:26–29, ESV

You know what's powerful about Exodus 35:26–29? It reminds us that God called everyday people to offer him their skills in practical ways for the benefit of the group. And even though these verses refer to different people's contributions to the Old Testament tabernacle, they illustrate how God has been working (and glorified) through practical offerings of willing people through the millennia. These verses set an exciting precedent for us in our God-given pursuits.

Over and over again in the Bible, everyday people are mentioned in big and small roles. None of them had any idea whether their work, their words, their responses, or their generosity would resonate through history, but too many times to count, we see God doing just that.

He brings eternal beauty from practical daily living. He wants to make our practical efforts online count toward his greater purposes.

It behooves us to let him make the most of us!

Let's talk of practical things. Some may be concrete and obvious; others may be more theoretical, but just as practical.

"Unpractical" practical practices!

Let's begin with some not-so-obvious ones. Not every habit is immediately thought of as being practical. Take these two disciplines, for instance:

1. **Prayer** Prayer needs to be a regular part of your daily meeting with God. Take all your concerns, challenges, fears, requests, and praises to Him. Include moments of quietness in prayer when you're not doing the communicating; instead, you're listening for His Spirit.

2. **Offering God your all** Repeatedly and genuinely, give your business or ministry to the Lord. Make a framed print with your mission statement for your office wall, if that helps you to do business and ministry for Him. Maybe choose a favorite verse that inspires your heart to endure in Kingdom-mindedness. Reminders such as these are practical ways to keep our focus where it needs to be. I've asked before on social media whether you have specific Scriptures for your calling, mission, vision in life. I have ones for writing, speaking, and #BeWorthFollowing. These verses keep me anchored on my life and work purposes in light of my ultimate, eternal purpose:

- Habakkuk 2:2 (MSG)—"And then God answered, 'Write this. Write what you see. Write it out in big block letters so that it can be read on the run.'" (Writing Verse)
- Ephesian 6:19 (NRSV)—"Pray also for me, so that when I speak, a message may be given to me to make known with boldness the mystery of the Gospel." (Speaking Verse)
- Galatians 6:4–5 (MSG)—"Make a careful exploration of who you are and the work you have been given, and then sink yourself into that. Don't be impressed with yourself. Don't compare yourself with others. Each of you must take responsibility for doing the creative best you can with your own life." (#BeWorthFollowing Verse)

If we're God's, if our business and ministry belong to Him, and if we need His armor to defeat spiritual warfare, then it stands to reason that prayer and offering Him all of our efforts would be the first, most logical (and practical!) habits to establish. Here are a few other ways to #BePractical that might not come to mind at first:

Develop the #BePractical mindset.

1. **#BeDetermined.** Common sense tells us that sticking to what's practical means having determination, a mind set on keeping on (#BeEnduring) as some of your efforts succeed and some don't. If one tactic hasn't worked, #BePractical and don't keep doing it. But #BeDetermined not to give up.

2. **#BeFocused.** Keep your business's or ministry's purpose at the forefront of your efforts. None of us can be all things to all people, and we weaken our impact if we try. Stay the course with your God-given dream, and you will see Him work. Fight the urge to comment on too many peripheral posts, and #BeFocused as you decide which Facebook pages

and Twitter users to like and follow. Also #BeFocused on how you use your time each day, avoiding rabbit trails that nibble away minutes.

3. **#BeOrganized.** An organized mind leads to an organized day and orderly business practices. Being organized will help your peaceful, positive outlook and your path toward success. Organization will help you keep up with who you've responded to, who is following you, and how consistent you're being in your social-media efforts.

4. **#BeResourceful.** Here's where the mantra "Initiate, don't wait" is important. One way to help yourself is to take the initiative and stay ahead of your posts. Keep an idea file of topics or even drafts of posts to cull through when you're low on time or creativity. Ideas can come from lots of places, but most of us need to write them down or they'll be gone from memory by the time we really need them.

A few favorites

A chapter on practical social-media habits wouldn't be complete without offering you some of my favorites. So here are a few things I recommend making a part of your work life. Have some fun with these, and use them to make your social-media success easier! They are not have-to's because none of us needs any more of those. They are creative tools at your fingertips.

1. Build fun into your social-media week! Develop a regular feature or two and name them so your tribe can recognize and expect them on a daily or weekly basis. Nothing extensive, these are quickie features that get you posted and in front of your tribe frequently. No doubt you've seen a Facebook and Twitter trend of "Throwback Thursday." Or how about

"Mood Monday"? Okay, that's a new one, but what a fun way to get everyone into the swing of the week by tossing out a Mood Monday question asking for input on how everyone's Monday started and what mood are they claiming for the day, despite whether they feel ready to take on the week yet or not. I know an author who gave her Facebook and Twitter followers a sneak peek into her real life by doing an occasional Weird Veggie Wednesday post. Her goal was to introduce her children to new vegetables, while also coming up with supper hacks for the end of a busy workday—something helpful for all of us. She showed a photo of the weird veggie, whether it was creamy mustard greens or roasted parsnips, along with a quirky caption such as "Weird Veggie Wednesday: Boys who eat parsnips hit home runs!" It had nothing to do with writing or books, but it invited her followers into her world behind the pages of her writing and gained a good number of likes and comments. Here are some other ideas:

- #MarketingMonday: Share a marketing business tip.
- #MakeItHappenMonday: Group members can share their one big goal for the week.
- #TransformationTuesday: How are you transforming yourself personally and in your business?
- #TipTuesday: Share a tip for their business or personal life.
- #WednesdayWisdom: People can share their blog posts, products, services, SM Post, etc. Something that they have that provides value to others.
- #WellnessWednesday: Invite people to share how they are taking care of themselves. What are they doing for themselves on a weekly basis?
- #ThursdayFunDay: Share a fun question to prompt interactive discussion.
- #FridayReads: Share about a book that has impacted you personally and professionally. Do you have a favorite quote

from the book? If so, share it. #FabulousFriday: Invite others to share their biggest success from the week.

2. If you're feeling stuck on one platform, try another to find an idea, and then morph it to work on the troublesome platform. What do I mean by this? If your blank Facebook status won't stop staring at you (taunting you!), move on to Pinterest or another, and browse your own pins or a topic you've been interested in. There are many quotes, verses, scenic photos, articles, and other great tidbits you can find related to your business or any old topic you're interested in. For example, if your business is accounting, look up pins on file keeping for receipts, invoices, etc. No doubt a bunch of creative filing systems will come up. Or if you're planning a business trip, browse boards related to your location. Add pins to your own boards and then turn that topic into a tweet.

3. Trying doing a series of posts for a platform or your own blog. A series breaks up one basic idea and expands it to cover several posting needs. You get more for your efforts, in essence. If you work for a youth ministry, you could try doing a series on technology smarts and write one post about some of the perks and risks of navigating technology, another on balancing online life with face-to-face relating to people, and a third as a devotional about going to the Word to overcome online temptations. If you're in the food industry, holidays are wonderful seasons for series posts. Early February is super for a series you might title "Cooking for Love." Posts can cover showing love through cooking, comfort meal ideas and recipes, cozy kitchen settings, aphrodisiac foods, plating and table setting for romantic moods, Valentine's baking with kids, and on and on. You can have lots of fun cross posting these in various ways across platforms!

4. Highlight someone else in your industry. There's value in helping your colleagues succeed. You can post interviews with people you work with, or even an interview with a friendly competitor whom you respect for one reason or another. How rare would that be? Find the right angle to make it work for both of you, and your graciousness and lack of one-upping will shine brightly to your followers and help build their respect and trust in you. Plus, you are actively fostering an atmosphere of service over selling. When it's obvious you care for other people, people will be drawn to good hearted-ness in a world that in many ways trains us to look out for ourselves.

Tips from the front line

Start your resource file of ideas for future posts. This is one of your greatest stress reducers! Ideas can come from everywhere: a walk outside, a new angle on a topic you read on someone else's blog, watching people at the grocery store, sitting on a park bench, doing your morning meeting with God in a new location, making a list of your best memories, etc.

Questions to ponder

1. Are you making prayer a regular part of your daily meeting with God?
2. Are you offering God your all? If not, what areas do you need to release to him?
3. Are you determined, focused, organized, and resourceful on your social media platforms?
4. What two practical steps can you incorporate into your social-media practices this month?

Tweetable moments

"God has been working (and glorified) through practical offerings of willing people through the millennia." ~@DrJenBennett, #BeWorthFollowing

"Prayer and offering Him all of our efforts are the first, most logical (and practical!) habits to establish." ~@DrJenBennett, #BeWorthFollowing

"Include moments of quietness in prayer when you're not doing the communicating—instead, you're listening for His Spirit." ~@DrJenBennett, #BeWorthFollowing

"If one tactic hasn't worked, #BePractical and don't keep doing it. But #BeDetermined not to give up." ~@DrJenBennett, #BeWorthFollowing

"Being organized will help your peaceful, positive outlook and your path toward success." ~@DrJenBennett, #BeWorthFollowing

"None of us can be all things to all people, and we weaken our impact if we try." ~@DrJenBennett, #BeWorthFollowing

"People will be drawn to good heartedness in a world that in many ways trains us to look out for ourselves." ~@DrJenBennett, #BeWorthFollowing

Chapter 11: #BeCreative When You Don't Know What to Write

He creates each of us by Christ Jesus to join him in the work he does, the good work he has gotten ready for us to do, work we had better be doing.

Ephesians 2:10, MSG

The sky is the limit on this one! Despite the famous quote's claim that "there's nothing new under the sun," I'm here to tell you that's simply not the case when it comes to social-media creativity. Social media has been a part of our lives for only a decade or so, right? Still so young!

But what about those dry spells we all face when we don't know what to write? Those are real. Sometimes the resource file grows thin while we're busy, and we haven't had time to brainstorm new ideas. Or sometimes our list of post topics somehow doesn't include one that really fits well enough with what's going on in our business or ministry. It happens.

One of the biggest struggles with social media is creating content that not only speaks to the heart of your dream client, but also speaks to them in such a way that causes them to take action, to engage with your post.

As I meet and chat with various business and ministry leaders, one of the hardest areas they grapple with is content; they just don't know what to post. And because they don't know what to post, they end up not posting anything.

Let this chapter arm you with some key truths that can make all the difference for you when a dry spell hovers near. I want to offer a "different" view when it comes to your social-media content, your posts. If you spend anytime online, you will find that the majority of social-media "experts" will state that you need to create posts that include:

- Humor
- Stories
- Questions
- Inspiration
- Value

And yes, those suggestions are great. But honestly, as Christian leaders, I think we need to go deeper; I think we are missing out on one specific area that can literally transform our social-media platforms while also transforming the lives of our community.

What is God saying to YOU?

Ephesians 2:10 says that our Creator created us to join Him in the work that He does. Did you catch that? We're not trying to figure out our own work on our own. We were created to join God in *His* work. We were created to join Him *in His creativity.* This truth is so freeing for us because it shows us our need to go to Him for ideas about the tasks He created us to do, including the content for social media.

Really? Yes.

So again, what is God saying to YOU?

Discipline yourself to meet with God before you get busy with emails, messages, social media, projects, and writings. Take initiative and set the tone for each day by spending some quality time with Him as He wants to guide your steps and your thoughts.

As I spend time with God each morning, He *never* fails me. As I read His word, He teaches me and shows me things that honestly are not just for me but are also for my community.

I often am prompted to post on social media directly from my time with God. As I read, research, study and am quiet before Him, He shows me His game plan. He puts things on my heart that are directly from His heart and that He wants me to meditate on throughout the day. Often those things directly apply to my life or work. And when He shows me these truths, I have to share. And if I'm honest with you, 95 percent of the time, when I share what He's shown me, it's those posts that end up having the biggest impact; it's those posts that get the most engagement. The more I study God's Word, the more ideas I get for social media.

Take this Facebook post, for instance:
"So let's not allow ourselves to get fatigued doing good. At the right time we will harvest a good crop if we don't give up, or quit. Right now, therefore, every time we get the chance, let us work for the benefit of all, starting with the people closest to use in the community of faith." ~Galatians 6:9–10

This morning, I'm grateful for this Scripture because it reminds me that I'm not alone on the days when I'm tired and just want to quit. On the days when I question what I'm doing and where I'm going. On the days when I wonder if what I'm doing is really making a difference.

Maybe you can relate. Maybe you too have days where you wonder if everything that you're doing and working towards is really worth it. You're tired, you're worn out and you just feel like you're not moving forward.

If this is you, here's something to consider. There will be hard days. There will be days when you question everything. But the key to getting through those hard days, is to always have the calling that God has given you, before you.

Write it out. Write out the calling that God gave you; write down everything you know about it, every detail. And then, put it somewhere where you can read it daily, especially on the hard days. Having your calling before you, it will always remind you of why you're doing what you're doing.

There is a harvest waiting for you if you don't give up. #BeDifferent #BeWorthFollowing

I already know what some of you are saying: "But Jen, my business (or employer) doesn't lend itself to posts like this." And my answer to this would be Yes it does.

No matter what kind of business you're in, you can take what God is teaching you and showing you and turn it into a post, even if you can't use Scripture. You can turn that Scripture into a post that still touches the lives of many. It's all in the words you use.

For example, when I share my #BeWorthFollowing message to a group of people who are not believers, or who cannot use Scripture in their work, I still share the truths of Galatians 6:4–5. I share things like

- make a careful exploration of who you are;
- what work you been given to do right now;
- don't compare;
- take responsibility for your own life.

Social media is about creatively stringing words together that "touch" the lives of your community. Gone are the days of writing copy that has no depth, copy that states the exact same thing that is on your graphic. Instead, we have to see social media as a channel that allows us to speak into the lives of others on a daily basis, a channel that allows us to share with others what God is doing in our lives. Ultimately, we write for Him. And when we write for Him, He has a way of using those words to impact the lives of others.

If you are a leader, entrepreneur or someone who has been given the task of social-media "management," don't take this role lightly. You have the opportunity to speak into the lives of thousands of people on a daily basis as a #DigitalMissionary. Your words matter. And I promise you, the more you make that time with God a priority, the more insight and words He will give you to share on social media.

Remember our verse, Galatians 6:4–5? #BeCreative and ...

Take responsibility for doing the creative best you can with your own life.

Tips from the front line

As you build content for your social-media platforms, one of the BEST things you can do is to create a Google document where you store the copy that you use for posts, along with links and pictures. I'm a BIG fan of recycling your content. This is perfect for those times when you have a busy week and you just can't create new content. Having a Google document with past posts, links and visuals will make it super easy for you to share content that you've shared before.

Questions to consider

1. What is God saying to you?
2. How can you take what God is teaching you and showing you and turn it into a post, even if you can't use Scripture?

Tweetable moments

"Social media is about creatively stringing words together that 'touch' the lives of your community." ~@DrJenBennett, #BeWorthFollowing

"Choose to see #SocialMedia as a channel that allows you to speak into the lives of others." ~@DrJenBennett, #BeWorthFollowing

"We write for Him. And when we write for Him, He uses our words to impact the lives of others." ~@DrJenBennett, #BeWorthFollowing

"No matter what kind of business you're in, you can take what God is teaching you and showing you and turn it into a post." ~@DrJenBennett, #BeWorthFollowing

"When I share what He's shown me, it's those posts that end up having the biggest impact." ~@DrJenBennett, #BeWorthFollowing

"We were created to join God in *His* work. We were created to join Him *in His creativity*." ~@DrJenBennett, #BeWorthFollowing

Part IV: Working Above the High Bar

The bar is already raised high for social-media success stories; what does it look like for you to run your online presence above that bar? Not necessarily in numbers, but in your Kingdom focus, your service, your heart for your customers. God sets the ultimate bar, and in His power we live and move above the lower bar the world sets, even though the world seems to want us to think its bar is highest and best. How can you encourage, not discourage, through what you believe?

Chapter 12: #BeClear
Maintain Voice and Streamline Content

The right word at the right time is like a custom-made piece of jewelry.

Proverbs 25:11, MSG

One of the keys for being effective on social media is maintaining a clear understanding of who you are and what your values are. No doubt you have found some favorite people to follow on your social-media platforms. But have you narrowed down what qualities draw you to them?

I spend a lot of time online, as you might have gathered, and I can't help noticing when something is working. In the noisy world of social media, here are a few leaders who have clearly stood out to me. There are others I could name, but for now these two stand out. Here's why:

1. Carrie Wilkerson, the Barefoot Executive: Some of her posts speak so precisely to her target audience. She clearly knows her tribe and how to connect with their world. Her Facebook post on February 15, 2017, referenced Mufasa's words from

The Lion King: "Simba ...You've forgotten who you are." Then she went on to tie that quote in with how often we struggle to simply be ourselves without trying to be who we think others want us to be. That life skill hits home with most of us on some level. She often comes up with specific, clear words for her audience that touch our emotions.

2. Lysa TerKeurst, of Proverbs 31 Ministries, knows exactly what to say to her target audience to connect with them. She knows where they are in this journey of life, and she communicates clearly to their hearts and minds.

People know what to expect from good social-media leaders because of a clear focus and purpose that resonates in every comment and post. So how about you? Spend some time with these questions to flesh out the clarity of who you are on social media.

✓ When people say your name or the name of your business/ ministry, what do you want them to think of?
✓ What five adjectives do you want people to use to describe you or your business?
✓ What five adjectives do you NOT want people to use to describe you or your business?
✓ What are your values? What is most important to you?
✓ How do you want to come across on social media?

Sticking to a clear, consistent strategy on social media will separate you from everyone else, in a good way. The last thing any of us wants is to identify ourselves with so many other people's styles and messages that we become inconsequential or unnecessary because someone else is already doing what we are trying to do, saying what we want to say, or posting content we wish we'd posted.

In order to stand out from the busyness of social media, it is vital to #BeClear about who you are. Let's discuss a few tips for ensuring clarity online.

Streamline!

Have you ever followed a blog for months because you love the focus, the content, the blogger's voice and personality, and the variety of the posts, only to find your interest waning for no apparent reason?

But this person used to be your favorite! You could relate, you felt like you connected with the other followers who commented, and you felt like your day was a little closer to feeling complete after checking in for a daily dose.

So what happened?

There may be any number of reasons, but one misstep that gets some bloggers in trouble and reduces their impact happens when they stray from their main message too much, offering too many opinions about too many subjects. If there ever is a time and place for sharing our thoughts about everything under the sun, it shouldn't be habitual from most of us on our social-media platforms.

I don't know many people who are experts on multiple topics, but with the ease and distance social media offers, it is easy to post boldly as if we are (and even justified about our own "rightness"). You may even know of people who give their views regularly on relationships, social issues, domestic issues, international issues, the US government, other governments, nutrition, medical issues, pets, public education, private education, homeschooling, working moms, stay-at-home moms, living in the suburbs, living in the city, the Democrats, the Republicans, the UN, big Pharma, the popular vote vs. Electoral College, and on and on. Phew, let's pause for a breath!

Remember discussing how, when left to our own wisdom unchecked by the Holy Spirit, it's tempting to say too much and get ourselves in trouble eventually? It's a rare person who remains unimpressed with themselves by having a following. So if our numbers are increasing or we're getting some very supportive comments, we can be tempted to assume our tribe wants more of our views on an increasing number of issues.

You may know of a few online leaders with huge followings whose own voices are crowding out their original and greatest purpose of promoting God. Now whatever they say may garner thousands of likes, but at what cost to those who are buying into everything they say as biblical truth—whether it truly is or not?

But we need to humbly take care and #BeFocused and streamlined. Remember Proverbs 12:23 (MSG): "Prudent people don't flaunt their knowledge; talkative fools broadcast their silliness."

We can lose readers by sharing too many of our opinions apart from our original reason for doing business or ministry on social media. Someone who doesn't take care with this can start coming across mouthy, and that wears on people.

Don't dilute your brand by writing all over the board.

Stick with your voice (and your own content).

Besides sharing too much about too much, we also run the risk of diluting our brand and weakening our #BeClear message by straying from our own voice. We discussed the subject of developing our signature voice in chapter 5. Now let's talk about sticking with it over time. Much like we develop and maintain our tribe's trust, we need to maintain our own voice that we developed.

We all have a voice that is (or should be) uniquely ours, recognizable. Think about a couple of your favorite bloggers. Isn't their voice in written form one of the qualities that draws you?

But it is easy to forget to let our uniqueness shine. And what a shame that is! We can read the posts of a blogger who has a huge following and try to emulate his or her style. But that kind of mimicry is obvious to readers, and it doesn't impress. In fact, writing with a copycat style actually can be a liability to our effectiveness because the original always sounds better, and because if we suddenly switch our tone or style, our followers may feel their trust in us shaken. In their minds, what else about our business or ministry (that they liked enough to follow) may change?

A related faux pas I see businesses making is when they copy or repost someone else's content more than coming up with their own stuff. Here are some examples:

✓ They consistently use the quotes of others instead of coming up with their own quotes.
✓ They use the quotes of others, without giving acknowledgement that it is someone else's quote. (If you don't know, you can always say *Unknown*.)
✓ They offer the same kind of *encouragement* that they see someone else offering who is getting some good engagement.
✓ They consistently *share* the posts of others without adding in their own posts.
✓ They offer the same *activities* in groups on social media that other groups offer.

Part of what it takes to #BeClear involves being secure in who you are; in fact, being solid with your personality, your gifts, and your message is vitally important to succeeding on social media. Now, don't get me wrong. There is nothing wrong with sharing the words of others on your platforms. I encourage it. But it can't be the only thing you share.

If you are consistently sharing the voice and content of others, then you are not giving your audience the opportunity to know you; and ultimately, you are not giving them the opportunity to trust you. If you want to be seen as the *specialist* in your field, then you have to know who you are and have a clear voice. When you do, you will connect with your ideal customer in some amazing ways.

Take the advice of Proverbs 25:11 (MSG), which says, "The right word at the right time is like a custom-made piece of jewelry," and offer content of gemlike quality. If you're wondering how to continually find resources for unique content, don't forget the last chapter—God speaks in fresh, unique ways to you. What might He want you to share with your tribe from those daily meetings with Him that is not exactly like anything else He shares with someone else?

One great example I've seen when it comes to the voice of a business is Hobby Lobby. This company has built a successful brand while sticking to its guns and the foundation on which it was built. They have a solid niche without compromising. Hobby Lobby does things differently. They've been respectfully clear about who they are, and that is to be respected.

The power of clarity

An Andy Stanley quote from a Leadercast session he once led stuck with me back then and still resonates today. During his session he said,

> *"Clarity trumps integrity. Clarity results in influence."*

He added, "What is the most important thing we look for in a leader? Integrity and honesty. But that's not who we actually follow. We follow people who are the most clear [about their mission and message]. Clarity trumps integrity. Above all else, leaders need to get clear about their company's mission. State it simply. Make it memorable—because memorable is portable. Get clarity around the idea and then infuse that idea with emotion. Then, don't 'how' the vision to death. It's the 'what'. A vision is not about 'how'."

Now, please understand that I'm not saying integrity isn't important; it's very important. But what people are looking for today is clarity. During this last, tumultuous presidential campaign, Donald Trump had a very clear message: "Make America Great Again." Nearly everyone has been able to state what his message is, even while his integrity was questioned time and again. President Trump consistently drove his message home. Not only did he repeatedly speak it, but he also wore it. Whether it was on his hat or by "expressing" his message through his American flag pin, he never wavered on his message. And this is what I believe, made a big difference for him.

As business and ministry leaders, we must have a clear message. Why? Because as Stanley states, clarity results in influence and people follow those with a clear message. Your clear message will set you apart.

This truth was something I pursued early on in my entrepreneurial career. As a social-media specialist, I knew that my mission was to help people #BeWorthFollowing online. This was what I based everything on when it came to my courses, consultations, client's profiles, etc. I wanted to help them be a business and ministry that others would want to follow on a daily basis. Needless to say, #BeWorthFollowing has become my core message, and still today you find me sharing this message all the time.

So, as business and ministry leaders, how do we create a message that not only clearly states who we are and what we are for, but one that also connects with those we are trying to reach?

Here are some tips to consider:

- **Make it your passion:** What motivates you? What are you so passionate about that if you could only share it in only a few words, what would you say? If you want your message to resonate with others, make sure you're passionate about it; it has to be personal.

- **Make it about the "what:"** Your message will come from your mission. Stanley states that we have to be careful not to get caught-up in the "how" but rather, focus on the "what." As business and ministry leaders, we must do the same. What do you want to achieve? "How" will flow from that.

- **Make it emotional:** The emotional element is what draws people in. Earlier, I warned against being too emotional in your posts. But on the flip side, be careful to show powerful emotions strategically. I'm writing this the day after the Super Bowl. Each year, the ads during that championship football game are legendary for their entertainment value. If you watched them, you laughed, right? Or teared up? Or at least felt your heartstrings tugged? Those ads are designed to click with people on a personal and emotional level. Your message has to do the same. What drives your audience? What gets to the heart of who they are and what they want?

- **Make it simple:** Your message has to be simple. And if you want it to be memorable, then simplicity is the answer. We take our memories everywhere we go, so simple is less cumbersome. You need your message to be something that others can "recite" easily. It needs to be short and to the point. Paragraphs and long sentences don't work here; they will cause confusion, and people will forget quickly. Making your main message simple will help you to #BeWorthFollowing.

- **Make it repeatable:** When your message is personal, emotional and simply stated, it then becomes repeatable. And the more you consistently repeat that message, the more others will too. It's been said that people need to hear something at minimum seven times before it sticks. So as a business owner, you must keep repeating your main message.

Remember, people follow those who are clear. So ask yourself, Are you clear on what your vision, mission and message are? If not, no one else will be. Instead, they'll pass you up for someone who is.

When you are sure of your clear message, you are one giant step ahead in sharing it effectively and drawing people in. Your God-given dream, this vision of your business or ministry, should be something you communicate with confidence. People are drawn to confidence, so be sure of your conviction—your message—and others will follow.

Tips from the front line

Questions to ask yourself before posting on social media:

- What is my goal/objective for this post? What do I want my community to get from this post?
- Is this post share worthy? If not, what needs to change?
- Does this post "speak" to my target audience? Why or why not?
- Is there some kind of "emotion" behind this post?
- Does this post have a graphic or video that unites with the copy?

Questions to consider

1. What are you passionate about?
2. Why does your business or your ministry exist?
3. Where are you going with your business/ministry?
4. What do you want to achieve?

5. Who are you trying to reach?
6. How can you simply state your main message so that it's memorable and repeatable? Think #Hashtag too!
7. How can you share this simple message in all that you do and say?

Tweetable moments

"Messaging matters. Your clear message is what will set you apart." ~@DrJenBennett, #BeWorthFollowing

"People follow those with a clear message." ~@DrJenBennett, #BeWorthFollowing

"If you want a message to resonate with others, be passionate about it." ~@DrJenBennett, #BeWorthFollowing

"Your message will come from your mission." ~@DrJenBennett, #BeWorthFollowing

"Your message has to be simple. And if you want it to be memorable, then simplicity is the answer." ~@DrJenBennett, #BeWorthFollowing

"If you want to be seen as the 'specialist' in your field, know who you are & have a clear voice." ~@DrJenBennett, #BeWorthFollowing

"Consistently share your message. The more you do, the more others will too." ~@DrJenBennett, #BeWorthFollowing

Chapter 13: #BeFearless
Dare to Be All God Created You to Be

● ● ● ● ● ● ●

God has not given us a spirit of fear, but of power and of love and of a sound mind.

2 Timothy 1:7

Have you ever seen videos by the Holderness Family? They're a family of four who make hilarious, good-natured fun of family life. They cover a slew of topics, and they've gone from being an everyday family of four to being a family of public figures who are even doing video interviews about making great videos.

One of their strengths is that they aren't afraid to be themselves, to look silly, to show their warts and all—while laughing at themselves and inviting others to join in.

And their following keeps on growing. After one day, their 2017 Valentine's video already had 758,000 Facebook views and 12,000 likes. Their website says they've been featured on *The Huffington Post, BuzzFeed, Mashable, Good Morning America,* and the *Today Show.*

When asked by a young videographer (on a video interview they created, of course) how to gain viewers online, Penn

Holderness (the dad) offered the simple encouragement to just start making videos of yourself, to see yourself on camera, to get used to it. In essence, just swallow your fears and doubts and go for it.

What do you have to be afraid of?

Let's face it, we live in a world consumed with fear. For one minute, turn on the news or scroll through your social-media platforms and you will find story after story that is centered around fear. From terrorist attacks, the Zika virus, cancer-causing foods, riot attacks, political worries—the list goes on and on. It's truly toxic. And if we're not careful, we'll find ourselves consumed with the fears of the world, so consumed that we will paralyze ourselves from ever living out the calling God has given us.

But even without external fears to contend with, all of us also have internal battles about our worth, abilities, failures, and yes, even successes. What happens if we find ourselves succeeding at something new, something that really matters to us? Even success can feel unsettling sometimes. What happens if we start succeeding, only to mess up and lose it all? Like tentacles wrapping around our insides, suffocating real living, we can be suffocated by our fears.

Where did fear originate, and why is it so easy for us to be fooled into letting it take hold and determine our mindset, peace, behavior, and goals?

Like all negative, crippling things, fear is a result of sin. Sin is a destroyer, so it's no surprise how destructive fear can be. But God is every bit in control of the universe and of our lives (and our business or ministry) as He was before sin entered the world. He offered the ultimate—His Son in our place—so we could live free of fear. And He puts His own all-powerful Holy Spirit in His followers to boot!

When we commit our businesses and ministries to God to build his Kingdom—first priority—"With God on our side like this, how can we lose?" (Romans 8:31, MSG).

Can I be real with you? If we ever want to experience the life that God has entrusted to us, we have to choose daily to do away with the fears that the enemy would love to strangle us with. As leaders, influencers and women of faith, we have been called to #BeDifferent and to #BeWorthFollowing, and as long as we allow fear to creep up into our lives, we will miss out on the opportunities that God is trying to present to us each day.

Remember what we've already covered about spiritual warfare? Fear tactics have long been one of the enemy's most effective weapons, which is why there are so many references in the Bible about not being afraid—in fact, those references are often commands, which means we're given the power to obey them.

> *There is no fear in love. But perfect love drives out fear.*
> 1 John 4:18, NIV

What 1 John 4:18 means for us as leaders is that when we know we are loved perfectly by our Savior, we're guided by love and guarded from fears of the world's condemnation and of our own potential to fail or succeed. Not that we'll never face those realities, but that "in all these things we are more than conquerors through him who loved us" (Romans 8:37, NIV). There are bigger things at stake than earthly wins and losses. Our God-given dreams are for His eternal purposes, and He will help us be victorious for those purposes.

Doing social media unafraid means:

1. **We must stop worrying about what other people think:**
   The one thing I hear from business owners as to why they are not getting active with live video on social media is that they worry far too much about what other people will think. They worry that they will stumble upon their words. They worry about saying the right or wrong things. They worry about how they look.

And it's these worries that turn into the "what will people think" worry, a worry that ultimately keeps them from sharing.

2. **We don't have to make things difficult:** The thought of social media, especially live video, truly scares some people. They worry about having the right equipment, the right lighting, the right background and the right tools. But truthfully, we are making it way too difficult. Some great viral videos have been shot with cellphones in cars! No studio, no fancy equipment, no touching up makeup. Move ahead with your idea, with the tools you have now.

3. **We have to be comfortable with who we are:** Can you see yourself free from worry about what people will think of you? Don't you think God desires for you to feel comfortable with who He created you to be? Your true, imperfect, authentic self. Far too often we try to make everything just right before we even think about sharing ourselves on social media. If you are real and authentic and have a message to share, the world will listen. And truthfully, perfectionism is the one thing that holds so many of us back. Aiming for perfectionism means that we are not comfortable with who we are. The fear of not doing something perfectly causes us to step back and do nothing. The world would much rather connect with someone who is authentic and not perfect. I've put this challenge before you in the past, but once again I want to challenge *you* to do a Facebook Live video. Why? Because if the enemy can hold you back from sharing your expertise, your wisdom, your stories, your true authentic self, then he knows that he can keep you from being used fully for the Kingdom of God.

Even so, I still struggle with fear every time I hop on a plane or drive some distance for a conference or speaking engagement.

The enemy tries to fill my mind with fears of what will happen if the plane malfunctions, or if I get into a car accident. What would happen to my family? All of that because the enemy is trying to stop me from fulfilling the calling that God has given me.

The enemy wants to make us forget that we have the victory in Jesus. But we know the truth:

> *The Lord your God is he who goes with you to fight for you against your enemies, to give you the victory.*
>
> *Deuteronomy 20:4, ESV*

You see, all of us experience fear at different points in our lives. We've got to choose to say, "God, I will not allow my fear of _____ to keep me from experiencing all that you have for me."

What I've learned through my experiences is that what we do with that fear is what determines whether or not we will allow ourselves to experience the good things God has for us. Fear is what ultimately holds many women leaders and influencers back from experiencing the success that is waiting for them.

Let me ask you, what causes you to be fearful? What are some of your fears that are keeping you from experiencing the best life that God has for you?

Let's look at the first couple of chapters of Luke, which tell the story of Mary, Jesus' mother, as she learned he was on the way. We don't know how old Mary was, but based on cultural trends, many scholars believe she may have been only a young teen. As was the case when angels appeared to humans in the Bible, Mary was "greatly troubled" (1:29, ESV) at the angel Gabriel's first words to her: "Greetings, O favored one, the Lord is with you!" (1:28, ESV).

When she was told she would have a child called the Son of the Most High in the line of King David, what do you suppose went through her mind? She was human enough to feel troubled at first, so it isn't too far a stretch to imagine her feeling overwhelmed but gathering her faith before responding with strength and grace: "Behold, I am the servant of the Lord; let it be to me according to your word" (1:38, ESV). And then the angel leaves, and young Mary is alone.

She may not have given in to fear, but I betcha it was knocking hard on the door of her heart, trying to rattle her.

She faced certain rejection from her people for what would look like sin on her part. She faced a life alone if her fiancé, Joseph, divorced her or, worse, pursued public punishment for her. She faced losing all of her dreams of home and family. And she did not know what her next steps should be. And her, why her? Why was she chosen for such a role? She wasn't royalty. She wasn't from a wealthy or powerful family. She had no reason to believe she was worthy of success, nor did she have a large tribe following her.

But God knew the calling he was giving her, and the success was up to him. The willingness was her part, and even that willingness was God-initiated in her heart.

Learning she would have a son was only the beginning of her story with Jesus. She had many days and years ahead that could have been overpowering in their fear potential. But we only read of her faithful commitment and trust in God. She didn't lose herself or her calling by letting herself be victimized with worry over what others would think or do.

We don't know whether she lived without fear, but we can deduce that she lived *beyond* fear.

Some Bible characters took a little longer learning how to live by faith despite fears that threaten. Peter, for one. Look at Matthew 14:22–32 that tells of Jesus walking on water. Focusing on Jesus, Peter was able to walk on water toward him until Peter took his eyes off of Jesus and began to sink. Still, Jesus was faithful to reach out and help him.

Just like Peter, there have been far too many times in my life when I have allowed fear to keep me from experiencing God's best in my life. How often we tend to react like Peter more than like Mary when we experience fear and we have no control over certain events, or even when we begin something new or step out in faith.

I can become fearful of things I don't have any control over. I almost didn't go to San Diego, California, for a conference one year, due to my fear of flying and earthquakes. And wouldn't you know it, my last night there, there was an earthquake and I felt my hotel building sway. Yep, I think God was trying to teach me something there. But when I look back on that trip, I would have missed SO many good things had I given in to fear.

Be fearless in pursuing what God has called you to. What fears are holding you back today?

- ✓ Fear of failure?
- ✓ Fear of what others will think?
- ✓ Fear of criticism?
- ✓ Fear of not being good enough?
- ✓ Fear of not being smart enough?
- ✓ Fear of success?
- ✓ Fear of others knowing about your past?
- ✓ Fear of responsibility?
- ✓ Fear of accountability?
- ✓ Fear of not saying the right thing?
- ✓ Fear of rejection?

You, unafraid

Let me encourage you. When Christ calls you out of your comfort zone, be willing to step out. Don't allow your fears to keep you from experiencing all the good things He wants to pour out upon you. And don't allow your mind to play games on you.

If you allow your fear and insecurities to keep you from becoming all that God created you to be, the world is at a loss. The world misses out on your gifts and talents that are so desperately needed.

Friend, we do not need to fear because we have the King of kings on our side; God has not given us a spirit of fear. And if we long to #BeWorthFollowing, to #BeDifferent and to be used by God, we have to make the decision today to not allow fear to hold us back anymore.

Take a few minutes to form a mental picture of the fearless version of yourself. How would you lead differently? How might your posts and comments sound more confident, proactive, encouraging, hope-filled?

Our unafraid selves are who Jesus empowers us to be. He died to make us whole, unhindered by fear. There is nothing about this world that frightens Him, no inadequacies of ours that make Him pause and think, *Hmm, maybe I can't make this happen through her after all.*

So go for it! Be the real you on social media, and offer what God has gifted you with and fitted you for.

So do not fear, for I am with you; do not be dismayed, for I am your God. I will strengthen you and help you; I will uphold you with my righteous right hand.

~Isaiah 41:10

Dare to BE who God has called you to be! Dare to #BeWorth Following!

The #1 Indicator of Fear

I've posted about this before, but it bears repeating. Sometimes we don't recognize fear for what it is, and we start getting impulsive and making changes that might not be wise.

Maybe you can relate to this example: You're stuck and you have no idea as to what you're doing or where you're going. You pray and ask God to give you clear direction. And after some time, you begin sensing that God is speaking. You feel like you've heard from Him and are understanding where He's leading in life, business and ministry.

But, after a few weeks or months, when things are not moving as fast as you thought they would, you start doubting; you start worrying. And deep down inside, you start questioning whether or not you really did hear from God. So you decide to "keep your options open." You start looking at other things:

- Investing in multiple businesses
- Choosing to work with clients who are not "ideal"
- Offering services you don't have the expertise in and things you really don't enjoy doing
- Taking on too many clients

Before you know it, you're stuck. You are not moving forward, and if you're honest with yourself, you just spent the last year of your life moving backwards. I've been there, done that. There were times where I felt like I had to have that "cushion," that security blanket in case something didn't work out. But really all it did was create more chaos, more worry in my life.

From the first time I read the last five words of these verses, James 1:5–8 always gets me to realize something:

> "If you don't know what you're doing, pray to the Father. He loves to help. You'll get his help, and won't be condescended to when you ask for it. Ask boldly, believingly, without a second thought. People who "worry their prayers" are like wind-whipped waves. Don't think you're going to get anything from the Master that way, adrift at sea, keeping all your options open." ~ James 1:5–8, MSG

Those words helped me realize why keeping your options open in business and ministry can be a bad idea:

- **You'll get stuck in the "Grass is Greener on the other side" mentality:** The more you keep your options open, the more you're left wondering if there isn't something better out there, something that will make you happier: a better business, better clients, better coaches, a better career, a better city, etc. And as long as you're thinking that, you will never reach your full potential with where God has you right now.

- **You'll settle for mediocrity instead of excellence:** If you're always looking for the next best thing, you won't be able to concentrate on where you are right now. And if you can't concentrate on where you are right now, you won't take care of the tasks that are in front of you with excellence. Instead, you'll do just enough until the next best thing pops up.

- **You'll lose your focus:** Focus is a good thing. Focus helps us achieve our goals. Focus helps us move forward. But if we're consumed with keeping our options open, we tend to lose our focus. Instead, we keep focusing on what's next and we miss out on the here and now.

- **You'll worry instead of having joy with what today offers you:** If you're always looking for the next best thing, worry will be at the center of your life. You'll worry about making the right decisions, what's around the corner, if you're ruining your life, if you've missed out on your purpose, etc. And as we know, worry tends to paralyze us.

- **You'll trust what you see instead of what God has told you:** When we choose to keep our options open instead of stepping fully into what God has called us to, we are ultimately saying that we don't really trust God. YIKES! Believe me when

I say, I've been there. If we feel like we need that cushion, then we are living by sight and not faith.

So, where does this leave us? It not only leaves us confused and miserable, but it leaves our online audience confused. When we choose to "keep our options open" and do multiple things and serve multiple people, we end up doing nothing well. And because we are trying to do everything and serve everyone, we end up confusing the very people we want to reach online. And when they get confused, they don't follow us or hire us.

I think we have to come to a point where we are not afraid to commit, to fully trust God with what He has shown us and shared with us when it comes to our business, our ministry, our life.

Whatever you request along the lines of who I am and what I am doing, I'll do it.

John 14:14, MSG

He's promised that if we will ask Him for help, He will give it to us. And if we will ask boldly and truly believe that He will not only answer, but will also guide us, then we have nothing to worry about. We can trust in His leading; He will not let us down. Don't be afraid to trust God and the specific calling that He has already given you. If you've asked and He's answered, move forward and let Him show you just how faithful He is.

Tips from the front line

One of the biggest mistakes I see businesses, organizations, and ministries do on social media is that they connect one social-media profile to another. Don't do this. Why? Because every social-media platform is different.

Far too often I see businesses sharing their Facebook posts to Twitter and the problem is that when you go to their Twitter profile, you see some of the post but not all of it, because Twitter is limited to only 140 characters. So what ends up happening is that Twitter then includes a Facebook link to the rest of the post. And when you see a Twitter feed filled with Facebook links, you know immediately that the person is not really active on that platform.

Also, during 2016, images posted directly to Facebook and not through Instagram were more engaging than images posted to Facebook via Instagram.[6]

Yes, you can use some of the same content on the different platforms, but do not have your platforms automatically feed into the other platforms. Instead, choose to post the content that you have created, on different days and times on the different platforms. And make sure that you are sticking with the character limits that each platform has and that those posts are truly speaking to your target audience on that platform.

Questions to consider

1. Which fears are holding you back from living out the calling that God has given you?
2. What one fear can you begin working on this week to overcome?
3. What friend will help hold you accountable as you step out and overcome this fear?
4. Have you fallen prey to "leaving your options open"? If so, why?
5. Do you worry too much about what other people will think?
6. Are you trying to make things more difficult than what they need to be?
7. Are you comfortable with who you are, or are you wasting precious time trying to be perfect?

Tweetable moments

"If we're not careful, we'll find ourselves paralyzed by the fears of the world."~@DrJenBennett, #BeWorthFollowing

"Want to experience the life God has for you? Lose the fears that the enemy wants to strangle you with." ~@DrJenBennett, #BeWorthFollowing

"As leaders, influencers and women of faith, we have been called to #BeDifferent and to #BeWorthFollowing." ~@DrJenBennett

"What we do with our fear determines if we allow ourselves to experience the good things of God." ~@DrJenBennett, #BeWorthFollowing

"Fear is what ultimately holds many women leaders from experiencing the success that is waiting for them." ~@DrJenBennett, #BeWorthFollowing

"When Christ calls you out of your comfort zone, be willing to step out." ~@DrJenBennett, #BeWorthFollowing

"If you allow your fear to keep you from all that God created you to be, the world is at a loss." ~@DrJenBennett, #BeWorthFollowing

"If we long to #BeWorthFollowing, to #BeDifferent & to be used by God, we must choose to not allow fear to hold us back." ~@DrJenBennett

"Dare to BE who God has called you to be! Dare to #BeWorthFollowing." ~@DrJenBennett

"Don't allow worry to keep you from sharing the message that God has given you." ~@DrJenBennett, #BeWorthFollowing

"Don't allow the excuse of not having the "right" equipment keep you from sharing your message online. Use what you have. ~@DrJenBennett, #BeWorthFollowing

"Be true to your authentic self, instead of trying to be perfect." ~@DrJenBennett, #BeWorthFollowing

Chapter 14: #BeSuccessful
The Priceless Impact of True Success

Blessed is the one ... whose delight is in the law of the Lord, and who meditates on his law day and night. That person is like a tree planted by streams of water, which yields its fruit in season and whose leaf does not wither—whatever they do prospers.

Psalm 1:1–3, NIV

A "worthy" dilemma

If polled, who wouldn't want success to be part of their life's story? I sure want it; how about you? At the end of my life I'm going to want to look back and see that I gave my all and lived and worked and ministered and led with excellence. I want all that God offers, the whole shebang. I'm willing to do my part, and I want His name elevated above all others, mine included.

I've longed to be successful in the calling, the assignment that God has for me. My goal has always been to make a difference, to lead others to Christ, and to really use the gifts, skills and talents that He has given me. But I'll admit, success to me has also included things like how much money I'm making, titles, and recognition.

When I entered the field of social media, I was quickly hit with the idea that success depended on how many followers you had; it was your "proof" of online success. And sadly, in today's social-media-driven world, I think success has become about making a name for ourselves. Success has become our idol, our identity. It's how we prove to others and ourselves that we are "worthy." And because of this thought process, I think we've traded a God-filled life for a life filled with stress, busyness, confusion, competition and comparisons.

We've fallen for the lie that success will make us happier. That success will fulfill us. That success will allow us to reach more people and help more people. That success will ultimately fill the gaps in our hearts and lives that have been aching for far too long.

You see, we've traded our God-given dream for the American dream because we've believed that the American dream will bring us happiness, money and fulfillment much more than what God's dream will ever give us. And if we're honest with ourselves, the American dream is all about what's in it for us, our selfish desires. Whereas the God-given dream is for the benefit of others, how we can serve and help others be who God has called them to be.

A Name in lights

Have you ever Googled your name? Did it pull up many links or few? Are you counting the weeks until your first Facebook post garners a views or comments number followed by a "K" to mean thousands have seen it, or your Twitter followers register in the tens of thousands? How about Pinterest or Instagram or LinkedIn—many connections on those platforms?

Numbers, numbers, numbers. We need people to hear of our business in order to stay in business. We'd like a certain level of success so we can provide for our families and give to those less fortunate and have the freedoms money can offer. And we'd like to feel as if we are doing social media right, if we're truthful. And if we're even more truthful, we'd love for the sky to be the limit for us.

It is tough to completely free our minds from the numbers game. It's tough enough to build a business, but the greater challenge may be building it without getting caught up too much in How Big Is Our Platform. Business is still business, even as our primary goal is Kingdom building. Publishers want authors to have big numbers anymore so they'll have marketing power behind any book they're taking a risk on, and we have to sell a certain amount of our product to stay in business.

Let's not muddy this: Reaching for higher numbers is a good thing, not a bad thing. Success is good, not bad. God made us to take His work seriously. If we Google our name and it pulls up a plethora of links (in lights no less) that testify to our work, there is nothing wrong with that. Hopefully that is one sign that we've had a solid work ethic. God wants to see us thrive and succeed. God wants us to use the gifts, skills and talents that He has given us.

But numbers have nothing to do with our worth. Zero. Zilch. Nada. The issue comes when success becomes our idol, when success revolves around us and us only, and we mistake success for value.

So, how can we #BeDifferent and move forward into the calling that God has given us, while also being successful for the benefit of others? Let's keep God's perspective on success. Aim high, work hard, pray always, focus now, surrender your dreams, expect His strength, live and work for Him, to see *His* name in lights through the work He establishes through you!

Let's chat about that by looking at a few stories from generations before social-media days—but ones that have gotten more views than any of us can begin to count:

Rebekah:

Isaac's wife and one of the matriarchs of ancient Israel. From all accounts, Rebekah was not looking for fame when the Lord made her the answer to someone's prayer. She was simply working admirably and sacrificially. For the good of others, she offered to do the huge task of watering a caravan of camels. Talk about rolling up her sleeves and getting to work! Through her, God birthed the twelve tribes of Israel. Any questions that God is the tribe builder, and He wants us to be available to join in His work that He initiates and accomplishes through us?

Ruth:

Here is a woman who had every reason to doubt her place in this world and every cause to crumble under a sense of unworthiness after the death of her husband rendered her homeless and without a career to support herself. Yet her unselfish choice to put her even more bereft mother-in-law's needs above her own earned her the reputation of being a woman of great worth, whom God put in Jesus' ancestral line. She lived boldly, getting the job done as needed. She was not too proud to do the nitty-gritty job of collecting the "extra" grains that were left, and she was secure enough to trust the Lord to rebuild her life. And in numbers too great to count, people have read of her grace and faith for thousands of years.

Daniel:

Daniel was a man who followed God, no matter who else did or didn't. He knew God's assignment for him and stayed close enough to the Lord (*three* meetings a day!) to soak up the confidence, strength, and faith to live according to God's definition of success despite a world outside his window that gave in and catered to what the world saw as important. God worked miraculously through Daniel's faithfulness and blessed so many others.

The prophets:

These guys had difficult jobs for sure, and most of them spent their careers as God's spokesmen without seeing numbers grow. Take

Jeremiah, for instance. His message was not what people wanted to hear. The only numbers he saw increase were those who rejected what he had to say. But he has a book in the Bible named for him because he promoted God's name above his own.

Anna:
Here's a woman who knew how to be truly influential. A widow of many years, Anna prayed daily at the Temple. Her top priority was to remain connected to God and take the concerns she saw around her to Him in prayer. More than anything she wanted to see Jesus in her day. And God blessed her humble, giving, selfless life by allowing her to meet her Savior on earth. Her name gets countless "hits" to this day as we read her story in God's Word.

The early Church:
Scattered and tattered, this growing group of everyday Joes and Jills faced endless setbacks, hardships and much rejection as they allowed God to change the world through them. And we believers are still helping build that platform they fought for so long ago.

Reviewing the lessons of Nehemiah

Consider other women (and men) of the Bible whose legacies were in God's hands. They did their part without knowing exactly how far he would take their efforts. *He has plans for you too!* He is continuing His legacy of love, truth, grace, and salvation through you right now.

I've written about Nehemiah in the past, and the lessons I still review from his life are worth sharing again. Nehemiah was a successful man who lived out the assignment he was given. Instead of having extraordinary powers launching him toward success, he saw the assignment God was giving him and he went after it:

- **Be open to the opportunity:** Nehemiah recognized an opportunity and grabbed it because he was moved by it for the benefit of others (Nehemiah 1:1–4). Success is always about the benefit of others. As Christian leaders, success always has an eternal perspective and result attached to it. Yes, even success on social media. Ultimately, our platforms and posts should point back to Jesus, giving people hope in the one person who can change their life. If we want to be successful in life and business, we must always have our eyes and ears open to the opportunities God is showing us, even if they are not what we had envisioned or dreamed for ourselves. The moment we close ourselves off from those, we start chasing after our dream, the American dream that will only benefit us (while leaving us stressed out, tired and filled with worry and anxiety).

- **Let your heart move you:** Success requires having a heart for what we do. When this opportunity/news was shared with Nehemiah, he was moved to tears; his heart was moved. He knew this was something he could not ignore; he had to take action. *Nehemiah 1:4 (MSG):* "When I heard this, I sat down and wept. I mourned for days, fasting and praying before the God-of-heaven." What moves you? What brings tears to your eyes? If you could change one thing about the world, what would it be? Far too many times, I think we get caught up in external benefits, things like salary, benefits, vacation time, retirement benefits, etc. And yes, believe me when I say, these things are important. But these things will not bring you "success." True success flows from being open to God moving us while being open to the things that move us. *Nehemiah 4:6: "We kept at it, repairing and rebuilding the wall. The whole wall was soon joined together and halfway to its intended height because the people had a heart for the work."* When you have a heart for the work you are doing, you will keep at it, even when the days are long and hard. You'll keep moving forward because your heart is in the mission and vision. You know you are helping others, that this "assignment" isn't just about you, but that other people are also depending on you to fulfill the calling God has given you.

- **Pray daily**: One of the KEY things that made Nehemiah successful was his consistency in prayer. He prayed day and night. He never stopped praying. And when we look at his prayer (Nehemiah 1:5–11), there are some KEY things we need to be aware of:
  1. *Acknowledge who God is:* Immediately, Nehemiah honors God by acknowledging who He is (Nehemiah 1:5–6). Give God the praise He deserves.
  2. *Confess your sins:* This one can be a tough one. When was the last time you openly confessed to God the wrongdoing in your life? In Nehemiah's prayer (Nehemiah 1:5–6), he doesn't blame other people. He includes himself and realizes that he too has been a part of the problem.
  3. *Remember the promises of God:* I LOVE how Nehemiah "reminds" God of the promises that He gave to Moses (Nehemiah 1:7–9). When you pray, don't be afraid to share the promises that God has given you.
  4. *Be Specific:* Again, I LOVE how Nehemiah gets specific (Nehemiah 1:10–11). He boldly asks God to make him successful. And he didn't want to be successful for the sake of being successful; ultimately, he wanted to honor God, he wanted to help others. That is why he prayed to God to make him successful.

- **You must have discernment**: We must be careful with the information we choose to share with others. And believe me, I've learned this lesson a few times. When God speaks to me, I immediately want to tell the world, but sometimes that really isn't the best thing to do. Sometimes, God just wants to keep it between the two of you for the time being because He knows the hurt and distractions it will protect you from. *Nehemiah 2:12: "I hadn't told anyone what my God had put in my heart to do for Jerusalem."*

- **You must believe:** There will be hard days. There will be days when you get negative feedback. But you have to believe that the God who called you will make sure you succeed according to what He's called you to. You have to promise yourself that no matter how hard it may get, you will choose to believe that God will fight for you! *Nehemiah 2:19–20: "They laughed at us, mocking. 'Ha! What do you think you're doing? Do you think you can cross the king?' I shot back, 'The God-of-Heaven will make sure we succeed. We're his servants and we're going to work, rebuilding."* And Nehemiah 4:20: "Our God will fight for us."*

- **You must put your fear to the side and remember what you're fighting for:** The enemy will do whatever he can to keep you from fulfilling the calling and assignment God has given you. He will do his best to fill you with fear. Fear of the unknown, fear of mistakes, fear of failure, etc. Don't be afraid. Push through the fear. Anytime he tries to bring fear into your life, put your mind on the One who has called you. *Nehemiah 4:14: "Don't be afraid of them. Put your minds on the master, great and awesome and then fight for your brothers, your sons, your daughters, your wives, and your homes."* God didn't create us to fail and He doesn't want you to fail. He has a specific calling and assignment on your life. Ultimately, He wants you to succeed, because when you do it brings honor and glory to Him.

So, how does all of this translate to your online platforms? To #BeSuccessful online, we must #BeDifferent by focusing on being someone who is worth following. We need to speak life, to share the love, hope and freedom found in Jesus Christ. God is showing you every day who you can impact online. Allow God to move you as you read through updates. Certain posts will fire you up and move your emotions. Pay attention to your emotions when you're reading on a social-media platform. In which of those might God want you to make a difference? God may be prompting you to share a different angle, to #BeDifferent.

I can't say this enough: Pray over your platforms. Ask God to guide you as you write, as you share, as you comment. Ask Him to lead you to the people who desperately need your words of encouragement. The more you seek Him when it comes to your online presence, the more He will give you to share and the more He'll guide you to the people who need life spoken into them.

And, don't forget to #BeDiscerning every time you're on social media. You don't have to share everything with the world. There are some things God would prefer that you keep to yourself. Remember, you are an online influencer, and everything you say and post can impact someone in a good way or bad way. Be wise.

Another part of being successful online requires that you believe in what you have to offer and in what God has called you to do? If you want to succeed, you have to believe in what you are doing, what you are offering, because the hard days will come. There will be unhappy customers who leave bad reviews on your social-media platforms. There will be people who mock you. But if you believe in God's calling for you, you will keep working and moving forward.

You'll keep on pushing through your fear. Putting yourself out there online for everyone to see can be overwhelming. Maybe the thought of sharing your story, your "realness," makes you want to puke. But here's the beauty of it: When you do, you invite others in to partner with you. When you share your true self despite your fears, you open the door to connecting with real people who want to get to know the real you. So do it scared. Push through your fear and allow God to speak through you online.

We've talked about a lot in these pages, and finally we need to remember a few other key points:

- Forgiveness is crucial if we are to fulfill God's dreams for us.
- Follow the call of God, even if you are standing alone.
- Get back up after failure.
- Arm yourself for spiritual warfare.
- Trust God, even when you don't have all the answers.

To be honest, this has probably been the hardest chapter for me to write because it's something I battle on a regular basis. My mind and emotions want to focus on what the "world" tells me success should look like, but as a Christ follower I know the picture of success is completely different. And not only the picture of success, but also allowing God to move me into something that, in the world's eyes, may not be considered successful at all.

I spend a lot of time online as a writer and a digital communicator. For the most part, this is a very behind-the-scenes profession. This may be where you find yourself also. And if we're honest with ourselves, there are days when we wonder if what we do even matters. Are we making any sort of impact? Today, let me remind you that what you do matters. Success for the online Christian woman carries with it eternal significance.

Success for the online Christian woman carries with it eternal significance.

What you write matters. What you share matters. The graphics that you create matter. The comments you share matter. Everything you do online matters. And every word you write and graphic you create is ultimately helping people draw closer to

Jesus. As Phil Bowdle, Creative Arts Pastor at West Ridge Church in Dallas, Georgia, says, "Create conversations through social media that God can get in the middle of."

Our goal in life and in the digital space is to always move people into conversations with God. We have such a unique opportunity to infuse hope into a world that seems to be screaming bad news on a daily basis. We have the opportunity to share the freedom that can be found in Christ alone. And whether you are a church, business, nonprofit or individual, you too have the opportunity to share why you have the hope that you do. Because ultimately, it's in Him where our success and fulfillment will be found.

Today, don't be afraid to let God share with you what His definition of success is for your life, your business, and your ministry.

#BeWorthFollowing!

By now I hope you feel armed with a toolbox to help you on your social-media journey. Tools like forgiveness, courage, discernment, a giving attitude, a God-focus, and realness will help you achieve your potential online and impact your tribe. Let God have the reigns of your business or ministry, and He will surprise you each day.

Are you hoping for success and trying to use social media to get you there? Does it seem difficult? Is it taking forever to build a following? Let me encourage you—stay the course. Trust God. Trust His timing. This world needs you, your story, and your dreams.

Seek God with every fiber of your being, continue being faithful to Him, and He will open doors of opportunity that no human could ever open for you. Opportunity will seek you, and before you realize it, your dreams will come about in ways you could never have imagined. And the impact of your true success will be priceless. #BeWorthFollowing.

Tips from the front line

Be real, be authentic, and engage. Your one goal is to connect with people to create a two-way conversation. Your goal is to #BeWorthFollowing—to create conversations that others can be and want to be a part of. And you do this by communicating in a way that makes you worth following.

If you want people to follow you, then you have to connect with them through your posts. If you want people to unfollow you, then your posts will be based on promotions and broadcasted messages.

Imagine a bullhorn. That is what broadcasted messages are. They revolve around promotion and constant information. They don't move people. Broadcasted messages are all about ME, ME, ME, not the people you are trying to reach.

If you want people to follow you, then your post will be all about the connection. You connect with people through emotion; you move people through your stories and insight. You craft posts that speak to them right where they are. So much so that they wonder if you were a fly on their wall last night.

Questions to consider

1. What does success look like to you?
2. Have you become attached to the American dream or God's dream?
3. Take some time with God right now and then write down all that He shares with you. Allow yourself to be open to His leading.
4. How can you increase your connections in your posts instead of broadcasting?

Tweetable moments

"We've traded a God-filled life for a life filled with stress, busyness, competition & comparisons." ~@DrJenBennett, #BeWorthFollowing

"We've fallen for the lie that the American dream is better than God's dream." ~@DrJenBennett, #BeWorthFollowing

"Follow the call of God, even if you are standing alone." ~@DrJenBennett, #BeWorthFollowing

"As Christian leaders, success always has an eternal perspective and result attached to it." ~@DrJenBennett, #BeWorthFollowing

"Be open to the opportunities God is showing you, even if they're not what you had envisioned." ~@DrJenBennett, #BeWorthFollowing

"Look for opportunities to speak life into someone on social media; don't make it just about you." ~@DrJenBennett, #BeWorthFollowing

"Have you considered praying over your SM platforms? Asking God to guide you as you write & comment?" ~@DrJenBennett, #BeWorthFollowing

"Let God share with you what His definition of success is for your life, your business, your ministry." ~@DrJenBennett, #BeWorthFollowing

"Seek God with every fiber of your being, continue being faithful to Him & opportunity will seek YOU." ~@DrJenBennett, #BeWorthFollowing

Endnotes

1   Batterson, Mark, *Draw the Circle: The 40-Day Prayer Challenge, (Grand Rapids, MI: Zondervan, 2012), 136.*

2   Ibid, 19.

3   Baer, Jay, *Youtility: Why Smart Marketing is about Help Not Hype, (Penguin Group, 2013), 30.*

4   Cooke, Phil, *Unique: Telling Your Story in the Age of Brands and Social Media, (Regal Books, 2012), 71.*

5   Baer, Jay, "How to Hug Your Haters: 3 Ways to Use Complaints to Strengthen Your Business," http://www.inc.com/jay-baer/how-to-hug-your-haters-3-ways-to-use-complaints-to-strengthen-your-business.html

6   Moeller, Susan, "The Ultimate Guide to Facebook Engagement in 2017," January 2, 2017, http://buzzsumo.com/blog/ultimate-guide-facebook-engagement-2017

Made in the USA
San Bernardino, CA
21 February 2019